# Ivan Moscovich's
## Mastermind Collection

# Peerless Probability
# Problems
# & Other Puzzles

Sterling Publishing Co., Inc.
New York

To Anitta, Hila, and Emilia, with love

Ivan Moscovich's Mastermind Collection:
Peerless Probability Problems & Other Puzzles was edited, designed, and typeset by
Imagine Puzzles Ltd., London (info@imaginepuzzles.com)

MANAGING EDITOR
David Popey
ART EDITOR
Keith Miller
CONSULTANT EDITOR
David Bodycombe
PROJECT EDITOR
Marilyn Inglis
EDITORIAL ASSISTANTS
Rosemary Browne and Laura Trenchard
PUBLISHING DIRECTOR
Hal Robinson

Clipart: Nova Development Corporation

Library of Congress Cataloging-in-Publication Data Available

2 4 6 8 10 9 7 5 3 1

Published by Sterling Publishing Co., Inc.
387 Park Avenue South, New York, NY 10016
© 2006 by Ivan Moscovich
Distributed in Canada by Sterling Publishing
$c/o$ Canadian Manda Group, 165 Dufferin Street,
Toronto, Ontario, Canada M6K 3H6
Distributed in the United Kingdom by GMC Distribution Services
Castle Place, 166 High Street, Lewes, East Sussex, England BN7 1XU
Distributed in Australia by Capricorn Link (Australia) Pty. Ltd.
P. O. Box 704, Windsor, NSW 2756, Australia

*Printed in China*
*All rights reserved*

Sterling ISBN-13: 978-1-4027-2745-0
ISBN-10: 1-4027-2745-3

For information about custom editions, special sales, premium and corporate purchases, please
contact Sterling Special Sales Department at 800-805-5489 or specialsales@sterlingpub.com

# Contents

# Introduction

Ever since my high school days I have loved puzzles and mathematical recreational problems. This love developed into a hobby when, by chance, some time in 1957, I encountered the first issue of *Scientific American* with Martin Gardner's mathematical games column. And for the past 50 years or so I have been designing and inventing teaching aids, puzzles, games, toys, and hands-on science museum exhibits.

Recreational mathematics is mathematics with the emphasis on fun, but, of course, this definition is far too general. The popular fun and pedagogic aspects of recreational mathematics overlap considerably, and there is no clear boundary between recreational and "serious" mathematics. You don't have to be a mathematician to enjoy mathematics. It is just another language, the language of creative thinking and problem-solving, which will enrich your life, like it did and still does mine.

Many people seem convinced that it is possible to get along quite nicely without any mathematical knowledge. This is not so: Mathematics is the basis of all knowledge and the bearer of all high culture. It is never too late to start enjoying and learning the basics of math, which will furnish our all-too sluggish brains with solid mental exercise and provide us with a variety of pleasures to which we may be entirely unaccustomed.

In collecting and creating puzzles, I prefer puzzles that offer opportunities for intellectual satisfaction and learning experiences, as well as provoking curiosity and creative thinking. To stress these criteria, I call my puzzles Thinkthings.

The *Mastermind Collection* series systematically covers a wide range of mathematical ideas, through a great variety of puzzles, games, problems, and much more, from the best classical puzzles taken from the history of mathematics to many entirely original ideas.

This is the 12th and last book in the Mastermind Collection. The great effort to include the maximum possible diversity in the selection of puzzles and related ideas in these volumes, is a tribute to early puzzle pioneers Sam Loyd, Henry Dudeney and many others, as well to modern puzzle and game creators with whom I've had the enormous privilege over more than 50 years to communicate, exchange ideas, collaborate, and create precious and enjoyable friendships – to mention just a few: Martin Gardner foremost, Sid Sackson, Claude Soucie, Mel Stover, Alex Randolph, Edward Hordern, Nob Yoshigahara, Jerry Slocum, Mark Setteducati, Dick Hess, Tim Rowett, Greg Frederickson, Jeremiah Farrell, Tom Rodgers, and many others.

A great effort has been made to make all the puzzles understandable to everybody, though finding some of the solutions may be hard work. For this reason, the ideas are presented in a highly esthetic visual form, making it easier to perceive the underlying math.

More than ever before, I hope that these books will convey my enthusiasm for and fascination with mathematics and share these with the reader. They combine fun and entertainment with intellectual challenges, through which a great number of ideas, basic concepts common to art, science, and everyday life, can be enjoyed and understood.

Some of the games included are designed so that they can easily be made and played. The structure of many is such that they will excite the mind, suggest new ideas and insights, and pave the way for new modes of thought and creative expression.

Despite the diversity of topics, there is an underlying continuity in the topics included. Each individual Thinkthing can stand alone (even if it is, in fact, related to many others), so you can dip in at will without the frustration of cross-referencing.

I hope you will enjoy the *Mastermind Collection* series and Thinkthings as much as I have enjoyed creating them for you.

—Ivan Moscovich

Often, our intuition is very good at solving problems quickly. See how it does with these two.

### ▶ WATERMELONS

*Watermelons with a total weight of 1000 pounds, of which 99% is water, are transported to a distant supermarket.*

*Because of hot weather and traffic jams, by the time the delivery truck arrives at the supermarket, the water content has dropped to 98%.*

*Before you make any calculation, what is your intuitive guess as to the total weight of the watermelons at the end of the journey?*

ANSWER: PAGE 98

## ▲ RAFFLE

*A total of 120 tickets were sold in a raffle for a luxury car.*
*The couple desperately wanted to win the car and bought 90 tickets.*
*What are the odds against the couple winning the car?*

ANSWER: PAGE 98

Probability is the likelihood that an event will occur. The study of probability deals with questions that are answered in terms like "possibly," "sometimes," "often," and "almost always"; in other words, terms of ambiguity.

## ❊ Probability and chance

Classical logic and mathematics taught in school tend to operate in an unreal world of utter certainty. Every question can be answered by "yes" or "no," and every decision is either "right" or "wrong." But in the real world few answers are wholly right or wholly wrong. The whole physical universe obeys the laws of chance. The seeming order of large-scale phenomena is sometimes simply the average outcome of millions of elementary random events.

That doesn't mean that any answer or decision is just as good as another. Most events follow the laws of probability, and if we know those laws, our chances of finding the most likely results are greatly enhanced. There are varying degrees of plausibility or probability for every alternative. They can be compared, their reliability fixed, and useful estimates can be made of the possibilities. This is the kind of logic that is developed in the theory of probability.

Probabilities can be measured, calculated or, when calculations are impossible, estimated. The result is a numerical value. A probability of 1 corresponds to absolute certainty; a value of 0 means the outcome is impossible. Values that fall in between give a sense of likelihood: 0.7 indicates something that is fairly likely, 0.1 indicates something that is rather rare, and 0.5 may indicate an event that is just as likely to come out in one of two ways, such as, for example, the toss of a coin.

Like all numbers, probabilities can be compared. Researchers use past events to calculate the probability of similar events occurring in the future. Such calculations play an important role in preparing for natural disasters. In locations where the probability of a hurricane is high but that of an earthquake is low, local safety workers can be trained in the appropriate rescue techniques.

In general, the probability of an event is defined by the equation $P = n/N$, in which N is the total number of equally probable outcomes and n is the number of specified outcomes whose probability is being calculated. In many games it is customary to talk about the odds for or against an outcome, rather than its probability. Odds are calculated as to n to N, so for an event that has a 1/5 probability of occurring, the odds are 1 to 4.

Even to mathematicians, some aspects of probability may not be intuitive. For this reason, and because of the enormous importance of concepts of probability theory in the modern world, it is imperative to learn probability and combinatorics as early as possible. The reason probability theory confuses many people seems to be the difficulty of understanding randomness. When asked, for example, to calculate the probability of getting a particular total when two dice are thrown, many adults would be at loss. On a roll of two fair dice, the number of dots showing can be from 2 through 12 (but these sums are not equally likely). The basic trick in computing probabilities is to know the number of equally likely ways an outcome can come about; this calculation is in the domain of combinatorics.

## ❋ Working out probabilities

$$P_{\boxed{\cdot\cdot}} = \frac{\boxed{\cdot\cdot\cdot}}{\boxed{\cdot}\ \boxed{\cdot\cdot}\ \boxed{\cdot\cdot}\ \boxed{\cdot\cdot}\ \boxed{\cdot\cdot\cdot}\ \boxed{\cdot\cdot\cdot}} = \frac{1}{6}$$

$$P_{\boxed{\cdot\cdot\cdot}} = \frac{\boxed{\cdot\cdot\cdot}\ \text{and}\ \boxed{\cdot\cdot}}{\boxed{\cdot}\ \boxed{\cdot\cdot}\ \boxed{\cdot\cdot}\ \boxed{\cdot\cdot}\ \boxed{\cdot\cdot\cdot}\ \boxed{\cdot\cdot\cdot}} \qquad \frac{1}{6} \times \frac{1}{6} = \frac{1}{36}$$

If two events are independent, the probability that they will both occur is the product of their respective probabilities.

$$P_{\boxed{\cdot\cdot}} = \frac{\boxed{\cdot\cdot}\ \text{or}\ \boxed{\cdot\cdot}}{\boxed{\cdot}\ \boxed{\cdot\cdot}\ \boxed{\cdot\cdot}\ \boxed{\cdot\cdot}\ \boxed{\cdot\cdot\cdot}\ \boxed{\cdot\cdot\cdot}} = \frac{1}{6} + \frac{1}{6} = \frac{2}{6} = \frac{1}{3}$$

If the two events are such that if one occurs then the other simply cannot occur and vice versa, then the two events are called mutually exclusive events. The total probability that one or the other of two mutually exclusive events will occur is the sum of their respective probabilities.

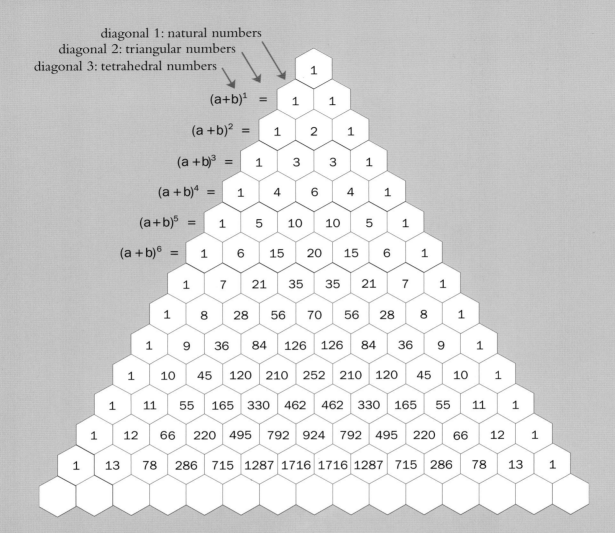

diagonal 1: natural numbers
diagonal 2: triangular numbers
diagonal 3: tetrahedral numbers

1

$(a+b)^1 =$   1   1

$(a+b)^2 =$   1   2   1

$(a+b)^3 =$   1   3   3   1

$(a+b)^4 =$   1   4   6   4   1

$(a+b)^5 =$   1   5   10   10   5   1

$(a+b)^6 =$   1   6   15   20   15   6   1

1   7   21   35   35   21   7   1

1   8   28   56   70   56   28   8   1

1   9   36   84   126   126   84   36   9   1

1   10   45   120   210   252   210   120   45   10   1

1   11   55   165   330   462   462   330   165   55   11   1

1   12   66   220   495   792   924   792   495   220   66   12   1

1   13   78   286   715   1287   1716   1716   1287   715   286   78   13   1

## ▲ PASCAL'S TRIANGLE

*One of the most interesting patterns combining numbers with geometry is the famous Pascal's triangle.*

*Can you discover the rule of Pascal's triangle (above) and complete its 15th row?*

*One of the things that makes the triangle remarkable is that the numbers on the nth lines provide the coefficients in the formulas for expanding $(a + b)^n$. For example (see 3rd row):*

*$(a + b)^2 = 1a^2 + 2ab + 1b^2$*

*Can you expand $(a + b)^6 = ?$*

ANSWER: PAGE 98

### ▼ HATS AND FIVE STICKERS

*There are five stickers, three red and two blue.*

*Three of the stickers are fixed to the hats of three mathematicians and the rest are hidden.*

*The challenge for each mathematician is to be the first to discover the color of the sticker on his hat (without looking in a mirror or taking the hat off, or some other such trickery).*

*Two of them make statements as shown below.*

*What color is the sticker on the hat worn by mathematician C?*

ANSWER: PAGE 99

Blaise Pascal and Pierre de Fermat created the theory of probability as we know it today. Their stories are as fascinating as the mathematics of probability itself.

## ❋ Birth of probability

One of the paradoxes of nature is that randomness is at the root of all that seems ordered in the universe, but it is only relatively recently (at least in terms of the history of the universe) that the nature of chance has been studied systematically.

Chance is big business today—it always has been. Since ancient times people have been concerned with, and curious about, chance. In many cultures the drawing of lots was associated with a form of divining, or listening to the voice of gods. The Old Testament contains many references to the way in which chance was used to make crucial decisions. Israel's high priests wore a garment with pockets for two marked slabs, with equivalents of "heads" and "tails." In response to a request for divine guidance, two "heads" would give the answer "yes," two "tails" a "no," while one of each would be interpreted as "wait."

The theory of probability has a clearly described and documented start. In France during the year 1654, gamblers often played a popular game, the rules of which were as follows:

The house offered to bet even money that a player would throw at least one six in four throws of a single die. This game was just a bit unfavorable to the house. There was a similar game in which the house bet that a player would throw at least one double-six in 24 throws of a pair of dice; this game was also slightly unfavorable to the house.

The 17th-century nobleman Antoine Gombaus Chevalier de Mere, who had an interest in gambling, suspected that the odds favored the player, so he checked his suspicions with the famous mathematicians Blaise Pascal and Pierre de Fermat.

Blaise Pascal solved the problem, and Pascal and Fermat later collaborated to produce the mathematical theory of probability, today one of the most important branches of modern mathematics.

## Blaise Pascal (1623–1662)

 *The only son of Etienne Pascal's four children, Blaise Pascal was educated by his father, who removed all mathematics texts from their house, having decided that his son was not to study mathematics before the age of 15. Perhaps that was the reason why Blaise Pascal started to work on geometry on his own well before reaching that age.*

*He discovered that the sum of the angles of a triangle are equal to two right angles, and his father relented by giving Blaise a copy of Euclid.*

*At the age of 16 he presented his first paper containing a number of projective geometry theorems, including Pascal's mystic hexagon. At the age of 17 he published his first work,* Essay on Conic Sections.

*Pascal invented the first digital calculator, called the Pascaline. He was the second person to invent a mechanical calculator. By 1647 he had proved that vacuums existed. Descartes visited Pascal but was not convinced. After his visit he wrote: "(Pascal) has too much vacuum in his head."*

*Pascal continued the experiments of Evangelista Torricelli (1608–1647), and from his observation that atmospheric pressure decreases with height, he deduced that a vacuum existed above the atmosphere.*

*From 1653 Pascal worked on his* Treatise on the Equilibrium of Liquids, *in which he explained Pascal's law of pressure, the first complete outline of a system of hydrostatics—the first in the history of science.*

*Pascal was not the first to study what would be called Pascal's triangle, but his work,* Treatise on the Arithmetical Triangle, *was the most important work on the topic. In correspondence with Fermat he laid the foundation for the theory of probability.*

*Pascal died at the age of 39. He was described by Donald Adamson in a recent biography as "...precocious, stubbornly persevering, a perfectionist, pugnacious to the point of bullying ruthlessness yet seeking to be meek and humble..."*

## Pierre de Fermat (1601–1665)

 *Born in Beaumont-de-Lomagne, France, Pierre de Fermat attended the University of Toulouse and moved to Bordeaux where he began serious mathematical research with his restoration of Apollonius's* Plane Loci.

*From Bordeaux, Fermat went to Orleans, where he studied law at the university. By 1631 he had become a lawyer and by 1652 he was promoted to the highest-level post at the criminal court.*

*All that time Fermat had been preoccupied with mathematics, proving geometrical theorems, and studying spirals and falling bodies.*

*His reputation as one of the leading mathematicians in the world was soon established, but attempts to get his work published failed because Fermat never really wanted to be published.*

*Today, Fermat is best remembered for his work in number theory, especially for Fermat's Last Theorem, written in the margin of a copy of Bachet's translation of Diphantus's* Arithmetica. *Fermat wrote "I have discovered a truly remarkable proof which this margin is too small to contain."*

*That sentence drove mathematicians mad with unsuccessful attempts to prove the theorem—until 1994, when Andrew Wiles finally proved it.*

*Fermat's correspondence with Blaise Pascal formed the basis of the theory of probability, and the two are today considered to be joint founders of the subject.*

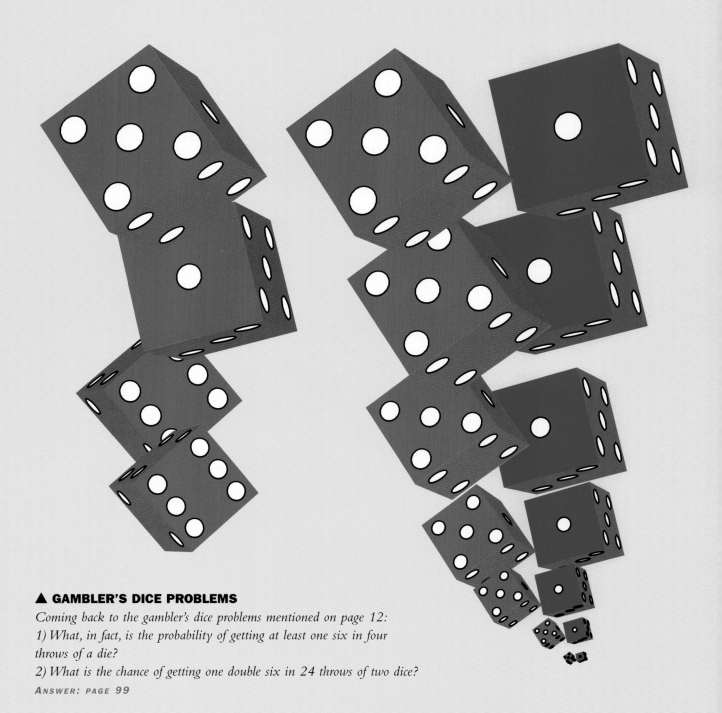

## ▲ GAMBLER'S DICE PROBLEMS

*Coming back to the gambler's dice problems mentioned on page 12:*
*1) What, in fact, is the probability of getting at least one six in four throws of a die?*
*2) What is the chance of getting one double six in 24 throws of two dice?*

ANSWER: PAGE 99

## ▲ THROWING A DIE

*Your friend throws a die, and then you throw the same die.*

*What is the probability that you will throw a higher number than your friend?*

ANSWER: PAGE 99

Sometimes what we think we see is not actually a true reflection of reality. Some of the signals received by our brains may be misleading.

> **All our knowledge has its origin in our perceptions.**
> *Leonardo da Vinci*

## ❋ Perception—the limits of seeing

We have five senses through which we perceive the world around us: seeing, hearing, touching, tasting, and smelling. These senses are not perfect and can sometimes fool us. Our brains have the job of interpreting the messages our senses send in, but some messages can be misunderstood so that we get a wrong impression of what is happening outside us.

We often use these misinterpretations on purpose. For example, a movie film only appears to show movement. We know that the pictures on the film are perfectly still but our brains are fooled into believing that we see movement when the still pictures are shown in quick succession.

Most people experience seeing as a passive "taking in" process. But in fact, perception is an active pattern-seeking process that is closely allied to the act of thinking. The brain is as much a seeing organ as the eye. Optical illusions take advantage of the tendency of the human brain to see things as it *thinks* they should be—based on previous experiences—rather than as they are. Although this normalizing property of our perceptual system is widely used in science, math, art, design, and architecture, the ease with which we can be fooled by a simple optical illusion should serve as a warning about the general unreliability of our observational skills. (Remember that if you should ever have to listen to eyewitness testimony.)

We can be made to perceive things to be larger than they actually are, register depth in a two-dimensional flat surface, see colors in a monochromatic pattern, or experience motion in a static image.

There is a limit to the reliability of our senses, and no amount of practice can ever make them good enough for some special tasks. One solution to this problem is to find ways to extend our senses, to invent devices capable of perceiving and recording information without error.

Although no one has created a perfect system for doing this, cameras and recorders have proven to be much more reliable and free from bias than even the best human observer.

The human tendency to be tripped up by our perceptions has long been a source of inspiration for the makers of optical illusions (and for "op art" creators).

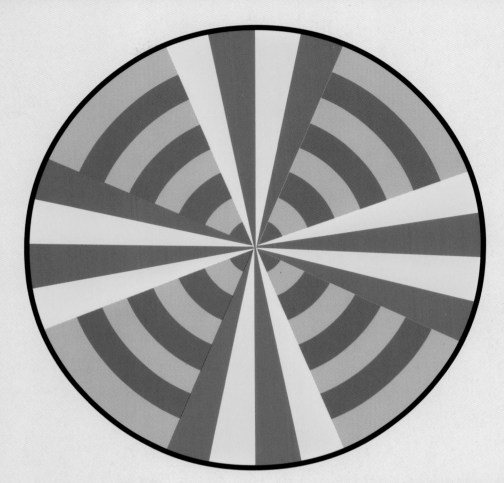

## ▲ FIGURE-GROUND

Most patterns have a figure and a background. When we look at a design like the one above, some parts of the pattern become "figural" and differentiated from the rest of the field which forms the "ground" of the figure or pattern. The figure stands out and the ground tends to fall back.

Is it an easy task to make a distinction between the two?

Can you find the figure of the pattern? Is it the radially marked cross or the concentrically marked cross? Or something else?

ANSWER: PAGE 100

## ▲ HOLLOW CUBE 1

*Imagine you are peering into a hollow cube from different angles and orientations. At the bottom of the cube there is a colored 7-by-7 grid forming a picture. Each time you look, you can see only a portion of the pattern. But from the six different views, there is enough information to reconstruct the entire picture in the empty grid provided at the bottom of the page.*

*What is the picture?*

ANSWER: PAGE 100

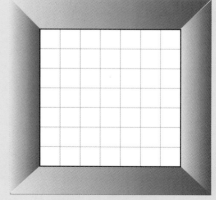

### ▲ HOLLOW CUBE 2

*The base of a cubical box is divided into a 6-by-6 grid and each square is either black or white.*

*From these four views into the box can you work out the shape of the design on the base?*

ANSWER: PAGE *100*

There are many problems dealing with coincidence. One of the most famous is the mixed hats, or mixed letters, problem, which is sometimes also called the "Montfort problem."

## ❈ The Montfort Problem

Suppose n men attend a party, checking in their hats with a checkroom person, who mixes up the hats. (In a variation of this problem, a secretary mixes up letters before putting them in envelopes.) What is the probability that, in spite of the mix-ups, at least one person will get back his own hat? Do you think there is a better than 50-50 chance of any of them getting his own hat?

The explanation of the solution is beyond our scope here, so we shall only provide the answer. The surprising conclusion is that, as n grows, the chance that any specific man will get his own hat gets smaller and smaller but there is a growing chance that at least one man will get his own hat—the two effects cancel each other.

The probability that at least one man will get his own hat is about 63%.

You can check the validity of this result with a deck of cards. Shuffle it, and then turn up the cards one at a time, counting: "ace, two, three, four…ten, jack, queen, king, ace, two, three…

What is the chance that your count will identify at least one card?

This is, in fact, the same problem as that of the mixed hats. The odds are quite good that you will have at least one match, and possibly more. Try it!

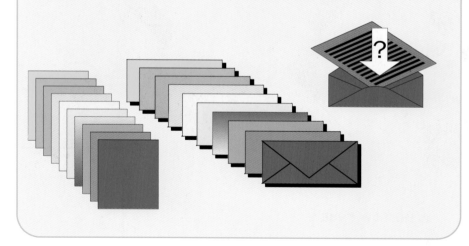

### ▼ MIXED HATS

*Puzzle 1) Three men check in their hats at a restaurant.*

   *A careless hatcheck person mixes up the tickets before handing them out. When the three men later call for their hats, what do you think the chances are that the right hat will be returned to at least one of them?*

*Puzzle 2) What are the chances for six men?*

ANSWER: PAGE 101

Illusions have intrigued us for thousands of years, and we delight in having our senses tricked. This three-dimensional cube illusion translates well onto a page.

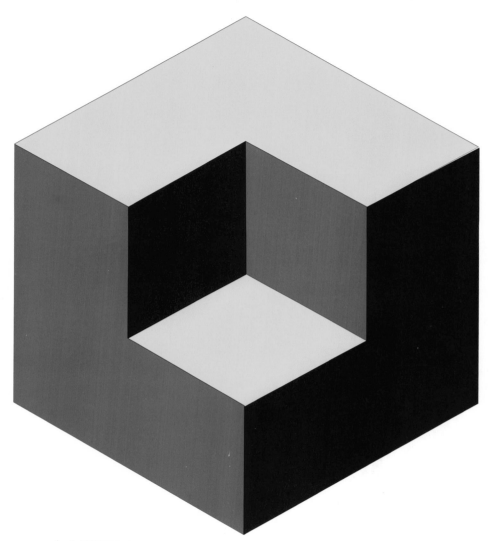

### ▲ CORNER CUBE

*Some three-dimensional illusions work as well in two dimensions as they do in three.*

*For instance, in this image, what do you see? A small cube in front of a corner of the larger cube? A small cube inside a corner of the larger cube? A small cube cut out of a corner of the larger cube?*

ANSWER: PAGE **101**

▼ **INTERRUPTIONS**

*Can you decipher the message?*

ANSWER: PAGE 101

Cubes and dice provide endless possibilities for puzzles and for games. The puzzles on the next few pages rely on both.

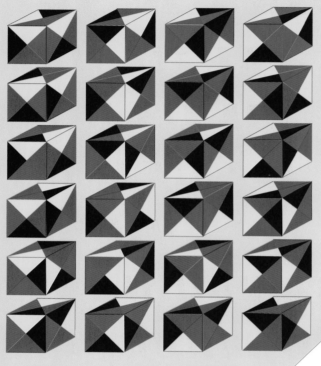

### ◀ ROLLING CUBE

*A cube can be placed in 24 different possible orientations.*

*This can be demonstrated with the cube pattern shown below on which every face has been divided into four colored triangles, and which you can copy, cut out, and fold. The 24 different orientations of this cube can be seen at left.*

*What is the smallest board you would need in order to roll a cube from square to square so that the cube would display a different orientation on each square?*

ANSWER: PAGE 102

COLOR CUBE ORIENTATIONS
Visualizing the 24 different orientations of a cube.

COLOR CUBE TEMPLATE
The template for the cube. Copy, color, and cut out, then glue together using white triangles as tabs for gluing.

## ▶ ROLLING DICE

*In 1963, Martin Gardner introduced problems with dice rolling around on chessboards of different sizes.*

*The die's dimensions are the same as the unit cells of the boards, and the die moves by rolling to an adjacent square, bringing a new face to the top of the die with each move.*

*Puzzle 1) From the position shown above, can you roll the die one face at a time six times so that it ends up on the bottom left square with its 6 facing up?*

ANSWER: PAGE 102

*Puzzle 2) Can you roll the die six times in succession from the top square as shown, one face at a time, to end on the bottom left square with numbers from 1 to 6 facing up?*

ANSWER: PAGE 102

Einstein

Beethoven

Stalin

Newton

Queen
Elizabeth I

Shakespeare

Portrait Cube

## ▲ ROLLING PORTRAIT CUBE

*Rolling cube puzzles were first mentioned by Dudeney in his* Amusements in Mathematics, *published in 1917 and later widely popularized by Martin Gardner and John Harris. The latter devising a new type of rolling cube puzzle involving tours of a chessboard.*

*In our puzzle a cube with faces of six famous people is rolled on a chessboard with two puzzle objectives:*

*Puzzle 1) Starting with Einstein facing up on the bottom left square of the gameboard, the object is to visit each square of the board exactly once, rolling the cube from square to square as in the rolling cube puzzles on page 25, and end at the bottom right square of the board with Einstein on top once again (not necessarily facing the same way). This may sound simple, but Einstein is not allowed to be on top during the whole trip, except at the start and end as stated.*
*ANSWER: PAGE 103*

*Puzzle 2) We have had too much of Stalin! Can you complete the same trip starting with Einstein facing up on the fourth square of the second row from the top and make a closed tour, coming back to the same square without allowing Stalin to appear on top at any stage of the tour?*
*ANSWER: PAGE 104*

| | | | | | | | |
|---|---|---|---|---|---|---|---|
| | | | | | | | |
| | | | Start and finish<br><br>Puzzle 2 | | | | |
| | | | | | | | |
| | | | | | | | |
| | | | | | | | |
| | | | | | | | |
| Start<br><br>Puzzle 1 | | | | | | | Finish<br><br>Puzzle 1 |

## ✳ Pi

The ratio between the circumference of a circle and its diameter is one of the most fascinating numbers in mathematics. The Babylonians gave the ratio as simply 3, though other ancient mathematicians strove for greater precision. In 225 B.C., the Greek mathematician Archimedes inscribed and circumscribed a circle with a 96-sided polygon and found that the ratio lay between 3.142857 and 3.140845

Ptolemy, in 150 A.D., found a value of 3.1416 for pi, which is sufficiently accurate for most practical purposes.

These days, pi ($\pi$), as that ratio is known, has been calculated to millions of decimal places. Why should anyone bother to carry pi to such fantastic lengths through the ages, let alone today?

There are three good reasons: Firstly, pi is there. It appears very frequently in mathematics, often in instances where its appearance is unexpected.

Secondly, calculating pi may have useful incidental consequences. Today the calculation of pi provides a way to test new computers and train programmers.

Thirdly, the more digits of pi are known, the more mathematicians hope to answer a major unsolved problem in number theory: Is the sequence of digits behind the decimal place completely distinguishable from a random sequence? Thus far there seems to be no hidden pattern, but pi does contain an endless variety of remarkable patterns that are the result of pure chance. For example, starting with the 710,000th decimal place, pi begins to stutter 3333333. Similar runs have been found for every digit except 2 and 4.

The ratio was named pi in 1737 by Leonhard Euler. In 1882 the German mathematician Ferdinand von Lindenmall proved that pi is a transcendental number; that is, neither pi itself nor any of its whole powers can be expressed as a simple fraction. No fraction, with integers above and below the line, can exactly equal pi, and no straight line of length pi can be constructed with compass and ruler alone.

The importance of pi lies not simply in its role as a geometric ratio; pi appears in the formulas engineers use to calculate the force of magnetic fields and the formulas physicists use to describe the structure of space and time.

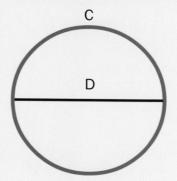

C/D = 3.14
Pi to two decimal places

## ▼ MEMORIZING PI

*In the table below are the first 2000 decimal places of pi.*

*Look at the table for five minutes, trying to memorize as many consecutive numbers of pi as you can. Take the table away and write down the numbers or recite them. Check your result.*

*How many numbers did you get right before your first mistake?*

*What do you think is the present world record for memorizing the digits of pi?*

ANSWER: PAGE 105

3.1415926535897932384626433832795028841971693993751058209749445923078164062862089986280348253421170679821480865132823066470938446095505822317253594081284811174502841027019385211055596446229489549303819644288109756659334461284756482337867831652712019091456485669234603486104543266482133936072602491412737245870066063155881748815209209628292540917153643678925903600113305305488204665213841469519415116094330572703657595919530921861173819326117931051185480744623799627495673518857527248912279381830119491298336733624406566430860213949463952247371907021798609437027705392171762931767523846748184676694051320005681271452635608277857713427577896091736371787214684409012249534301465495853710507922796892589235420199561121290219608640344181598136297747713099605187072113499999983729780499510597317328160963185950244594553469083026425223082533446850352619311881710100031378387528865875332083814206171776691473035982534904287554687311595628638823537875937519577818577805321712268066130019278766111959092164201989380952572010654858632788659361533818279682303019520353018529689957736225994138912497217752834791315155748572424541506959508295331168617278558890750983817546374649393192550604009277016711390098488240128583616035637076601047101819429555961989467678374494482553797747268471040475346462080466842590694912933136770289891521047521620569660240580381501935112533824300355876402474964732639141992726042699227967823547816360093417216412199245863150302861829745557067498385054945885869269956909272107975093029553211653449872027559602364806654991198818347977535663698074265425278625518184175746728909777727938000816470600161452491921732172147723501414419735685481613611573525521334757418494684385233239073941433345477624168625189835694855620992192221842725502542568876717904946016534668049886272327917860857843838279679766814541009538837863609506800642251252051173929848960841284886269456042419652850222106611863067442786220391949450471237137869609563643719172874677646575739624138908658326459958133904780275901

## Georges-Louis Leclerc, Comte de Buffon (1707–1788)

*Buffon's Needle (described below) is one of the oldest problems in the field of geometrical probability. George-Louis Leclerc, Comte de Buffon, in his* Historie Naturelle, *a 44-volume encyclopedia, described everything known about the natural world. In the appendix he included the problem (completely unrelated to natural history) of the needle experiment. In his* Les Epoques de la Nature, *he suggested that the planet was much older than the 6,000 years old proclaimed by the church. He became the most important natural historian of his time, having great influence across a wide scientific field. At the age of 20, Buffon discovered the binomial theorem, and later introduced differential and integral calculus into probability theory.*

### ▶ THROWING NEEDLES

*This is a version of the famous Buffon's Needle experiment which you can easily perform yourself and which will allow you to calculate pi with fair accuracy.*

*Georges-Louis Leclerc, a French mathematician, showed that if a needle is dropped from a random height on a piece of paper covered with parallel lines, the length of the needle being equal to the distance between the lines, then the probability of the needle falling across a line is equal to 2/pi.*

*If the needle is shorter than the distance between the lines, then the probability that the needle will fall across a line is 2c/pi × a, where a is the distance between lines, and c is the length of the needle.*

*Thus, by throwing the needle at random a large number of times (N) and counting the number (m) of times the needle falls on a line, we can calculate an experimental value of pi as:*

*(2c × N)/a × m or 2N/m if c = a*

*At first it seems almost magical that the answer involves pi.*

*In 1901, Lazzarini, an Italian mathematician, patiently made 3,408 throws in the course of such an experiment, obtaining a value for pi of 3.1415929, a result with an error of only 0.0000003.*

*Compare your results with the results of the author's experiment, listed in the box on the opposite page.*

length of the matchstick or needle

*If a needle is dropped from a considerable height on our gameboard, a surface on which parallel lines are drawn so that the distance between them is equal to the length of the matchstick shown, what is the chance that the needle will fall touching a line? Compare your results with the chart below.*

| N throws | Matches falling on a line | 2N/m |
|---|---|---|
| 10 | 5 | 4 |
| 20 | 12 | 3.3333 |
| 30 | 17 | 3.5294 |
| 40 | 23 | 3.4782 |
| 50 | 30 | 3.3333 |
| 60 | 36 | 3.3333 |
| 70 | 42 | 3.3333 |
| 80 | 48 | 3.3333 |
| 90 | 56 | 3.2148 |

### ▲ UPSTAIRS, DOWNSTAIRS

*Which fly is higher—the one at the top of the page or the one at the bottom?*

ANSWER: PAGE 105

## ▼ RED CIRCLE?

*In this illusion, the circle seems to be crimped at the points where it touches the yellow triangle. But is it? And is it actually a circle?*

ANSWER: PAGE 105

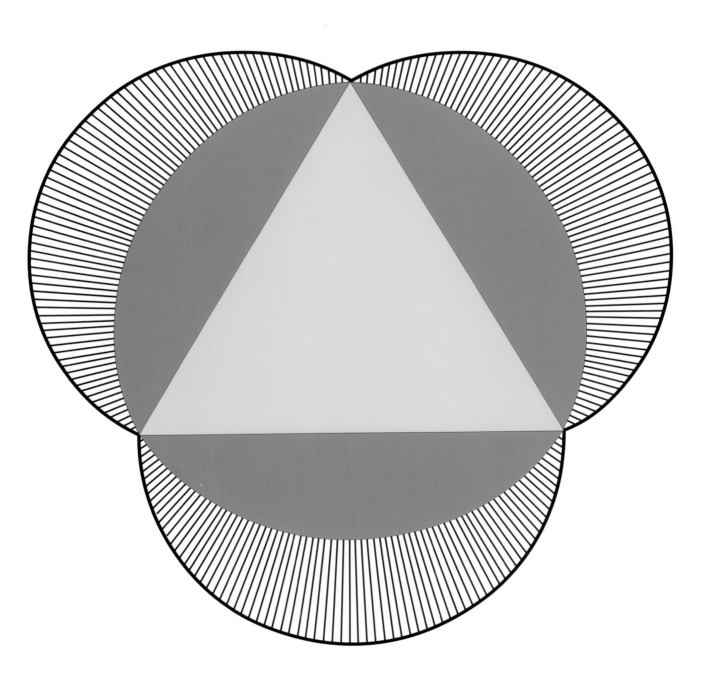

The next two puzzles ask you to connect the dots—but not in any way that you've been asked before. Follow the directions and see if you come up with a general rule for joining the points.

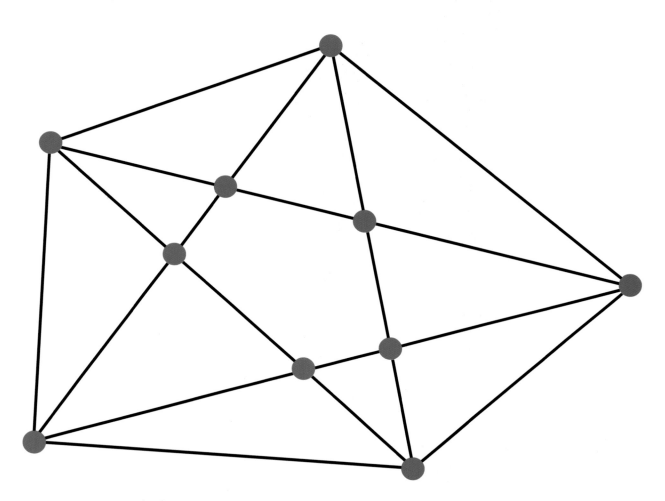

### ▲ TEN LINES, TEN POINTS

*In the illustration above there are ten lines forming ten intersections.*

*Five of the lines intersect other lines at two points, and the other five lines intersect other lines at four points. These intersections happen at places where four lines meet and places where two lines meet.*

*Can you form a different distribution of the same number of points and lines so that there are three points on each line at places where three lines intersect? (There may be other intersections that do not involve exactly three lines; you may ignore those.)*

*ANSWER: PAGE 105*

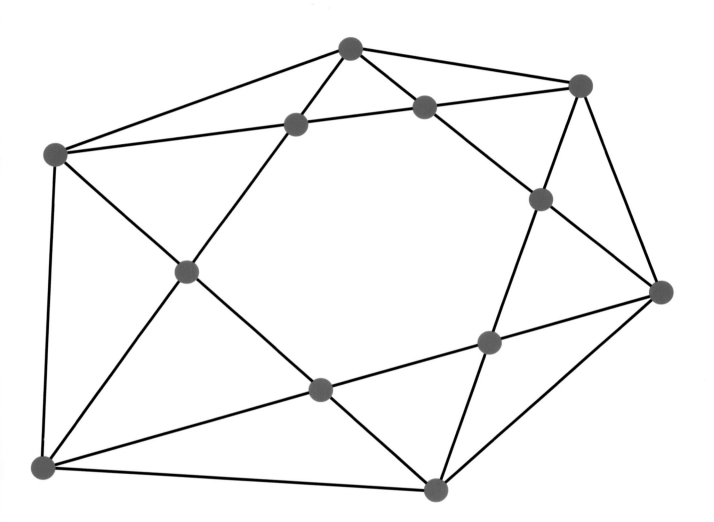

## ▲ TWELVE LINES, TWELVE POINTS

*Can you form graphs according to the same rules as on the previous page for:*
*Puzzle 1) 12 lines and 12 points?*
*Puzzle 2) 14 lines and 14 points?*
*Puzzle 3) 16 lines and 16 points?*

Answer: page 106

## ▲ ROULETTE

*Is there a sure way to win at roulette?*

ANSWER: PAGE *106*

▼ **LOADED DICE**

*How can casino operators quickly and easily detect loaded dice?*

ANSWER: PAGE 107

? **DID YOU KNOW?**

Princesses of ancient Egypt, 5000 years ago, were buried with sets of dice to amuse them on their journey through the land of the dead.

## ✳ Probability in law

Long ago, people would sometimes cast lots to decide if someone was innocent or guilty of a criminal act.

Rabelais's fictional Judge Bridlegoose decided lawsuits by throwing dice and was famous for his fairness until his eyesight prevented him from reading the spots on the dice accurately.

Marquis de Condorset implemented more serious ideas concerning using the theories of probability to improve decisions of courts of law. He suggested that a court should be made up of a large number of judges so that prejudiced opinions would be balanced out.

## ❄ More probability in law

It was not so long ago that the modern theory of probability was used as a deciding factor in convicting criminals in court.

In 1964, an old woman was mugged in an alley. A witness saw a blond girl with a ponytail run out of the alley and get into a yellow car driven by a bearded black man. Police later arrested a married couple who fitted the description and also owned a yellow car.

The evidence, though strong, was circumstantial. The jury convicted the couple of robbery, because the prosecution invoked a totally new test of circumstantial evidence—the laws of statistical probability—stressing the improbability that at the time of the crime there could be two couples as distinctive as the two accused in a yellow car.

The prosecution explained how mathematicians calculate the probability that a whole set of possibilities will occur at once. Take, for example, three abstract possibilities, A, B, and C. Assign to each a hypothetical probability. Then the odds against A, B, and C occurring together are the products of their total probabilities.

In this case, six known factors were considered: a blond white woman, a ponytail hairdo, a bearded man, a black man, a yellow car, an interracial couple. Multiplied together the factors produced the odds of 1 to 12 million that the accused couple could have been duplicated at the time of the crime. Subsequently they were convicted, receiving a sentence of one year.

Afternote: Four years later, the court reversed the decision, after a judge less ignorant of probability persuaded the court that the estimate should have been only about 41 in 100.

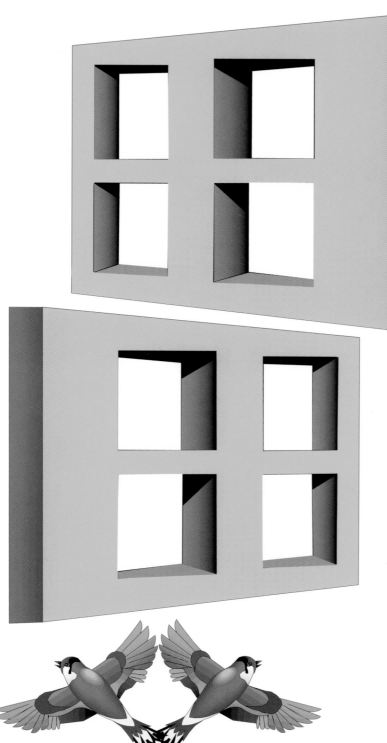

### ▲ ROTATING WINDOW

*Copy, cut out, and glue together the front and the back of the trapezoidal window, and the front and back of the bird. Before gluing, attach the bird to the window with an unbent paperclip as shown.*

*Hang the structure by a piece of thread and let it slowly revolve; look at it from a distance with one eye closed.*

*What do you think you will see after a few seconds? You will be surprised!*

ANSWER: PAGE 107

### ▲ MATH PANEL

*On a panel of seven famous mathematicians, three have beards. The seven mathematicians are to be seated in a line down the length of a long table.*

*What is the probability that the three people with beards will happen to end up sitting next to each other?*

ANSWER: PAGE 107

It seems likely that the probability of having a boy is the same as having a girl, but is this truly the case? See how this question is applied to two different sets of family groups in the following puzzles.

### ▲ TWO FAMILIES

*There are two families, with eight boys in one and eight girls in the other. Since the probability of a child being a boy or girl is about 50-50, would you think in families of this size that having four girls and four boys should be much more likely?*

*Exactly how do the probabilities of a family having eight girls and a family having four girls and four boys compare?*

ANSWER: PAGE 107

▼ **TWO-CHILD FAMILIES**

*A woman and a man each have two children.*
*At least one of the woman's children is a boy.*
*The man's older child is a boy.*
*Are the chances equal that the woman and man each have two boys?*

ANSWER: PAGE 108

**D**oes lightning strike twice? Are you safe in a spot that has been hit by lightning before? Read the following page and be surprised at the answers.

## ✳ Shell haven

An old wartime story describes a sailor who put his head through a hole made in the side of his warship by an enemy shell and kept it there during the rest of the sea battle. His assumption was that the odds had to be small that another shell would hit the same spot, which is, of course, a complete fallacy.

Each time a random phenomenon occurs, the probability of any specific result occurring is always exactly the same. Even after a spot has been hit, it is just as likely as any other spot to be hit again by another shell.

## ▲ BEST CANDIDATE

*You want to choose the best of 100 candidates for an important position. Second best won't do! If you choose someone at random, the chance that he or she will be the best candidate is, of course, one in a hundred.*

*So you will have to interview the candidates one by one. After you interview each applicant, you will have to decide if he or she is the best, even if there are still some candidates not yet interviewed. But there is a complication—once you decide against a candidate he or she is lost to you forever.*

*What strategy can you use to maximize your chances of finding the best candidate under such circumstances?*

*You could take a sample group of ten candidates, giving each a grade on a scale of one to ten, and then choose the first who comes along with a higher grade than any in the sample group of ten. Using this method you have one chance in four of choosing the best of the 100—better than the initial 1 in 100, but still a risky strategy.*

*How many candidates should you interview and grade before you choose the next person who is better than all the previous candidates? Using your intuition, can you figure out a way to improve your chance of choosing the best candidate?*

ANSWER: PAGE 108

### ▲ THROWING A SIX

*What is the probability of throwing a six at least once if you throw one die six times?*

ANSWER: PAGE *108*

## ▼ SIX TOSSES

*If you toss a die six times, what is the probability that each face will turn up exactly once in the six tosses?*

ANSWER: PAGE 108

## ▲ ROTATING SPIRAL

*In the early 19th century, Robert Adams experienced a strong motion aftereffect when staring at a waterfall for a few seconds, and then shifting his gaze at his surroundings. Everything seemed to be moving away from him.*

*A similar effect can be achieved by staring at a rotating spiral like the one shown right. (You will need to rotate the spiral by hand to experience the effect.)*

*Depending on the direction of the spin the spiral will seem to be either moving away from you or towards you. Stare at the center of the rotating spiral for 30 seconds and then look at the picture of the ship.*

*What effect will you experience?*

ANSWER: PAGE *109*

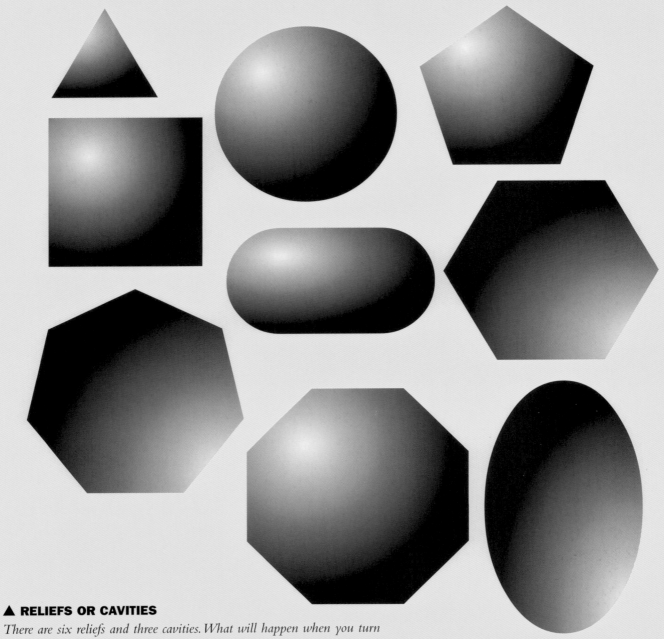

### ▲ RELIEFS OR CAVITIES

*There are six reliefs and three cavities. What will happen when you turn the page upside down?*

*Optical illusions are good demonstrations of the difference between seeing and perceiving. We never experience absolute reality. Our brains create what we perceive from a blend of external stimuli and our expectations based on past experience.*

*Our past experience tells us that light sources usually come from above, and we see reliefs and cavities accordingly.*

ANSWER: PAGE 109

**I**n many games, dice are thrown in pairs with the goal of achieving a desired total. The following puzzle asks you to calculate the probability of getting a particular sum when two dice are thrown.

▶ **PAIR OF DICE**

*"Chance favors the prepared mind,"* said Louis Pasteur in 1854. *That is true. When asked to calculate the probability of getting a particular sum when two dice are thrown, many adults are at a complete loss. It helps to imagine that the two dice are different colors.*

*Puzzle 1) The great mathematician and philosopher Gottfried Leibniz thought that the probabilities of throwing 11 and 12 with two dice were the same, because, he thought, there was only one way to throw each (a 5 and 6 for 11, and a pair of sixes for 12). What was wrong with his reasoning?*

ANSWER: PAGE 109

*Puzzle 2) Throw a pair of dice. What is the probability that an even number will come up as the total? Is an even or an odd total equally likely to come up?*

*What we know initially is that the possible totals can be from 2 to 12. Using the chart on the opposite page, can you work out the number of ways even and odd totals can come up when throwing two dice?*

ANSWER: PAGE 109

*All possible combinations of two dice to make different totals between 2 and 12 can be represented by columns in a chart. This will result in a distribution graph which will approximate the famous "normal distribution" or "Gauss curve."*

*We all know that when the odds of something occurring are 50-50, then half of the time, on average, that event will happen. But fewer of us might realize that the average usually nears 50 percent only after a very large number of events.*

*How large does the number of events have to be to rely on probabilistic forecasts?*

*You can check this yourself with a little experimentation (and patience).*

*Throw a pair of dice 108 times (3 × 36) and compare the outcome of your experimental evaluation of the frequency distribution of the throws with the probabilistic forecast visualized in the chart: the inner graph (represented by the dice) is for 36 throws, while the outer graph is for 108 throws.*

*After each throw color one square in the appropriate column. You may be surprised that even such a relatively small number of events can give a good approximation of the theory. The red graph is the result of the author's experiment. Try it yourself!*

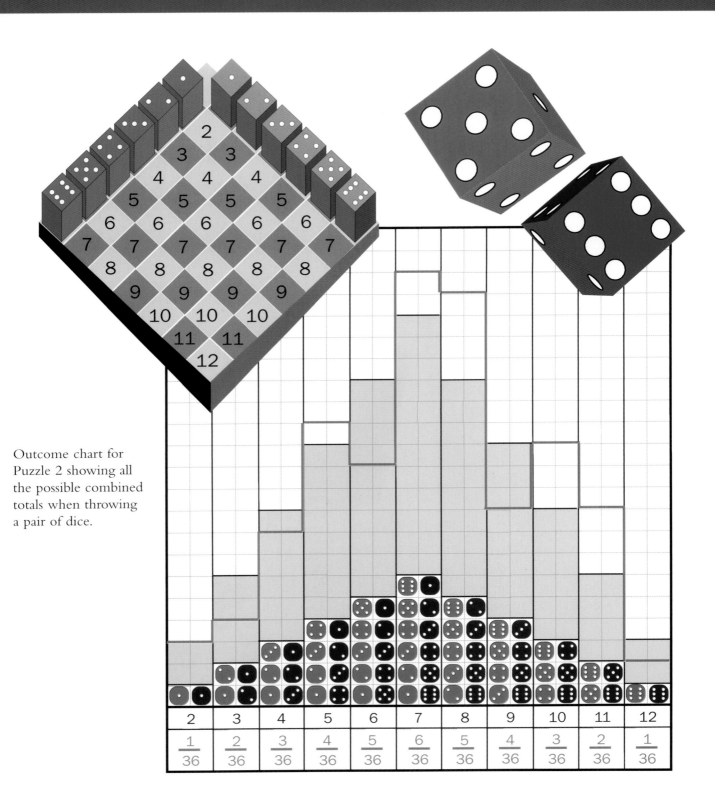

Outcome chart for Puzzle 2 showing all the possible combined totals when throwing a pair of dice.

| 2 | 3 | 4 | 5 | 6 | 7 | 8 | 9 | 10 | 11 | 12 |
|---|---|---|---|---|---|---|---|---|---|---|
| $\frac{1}{36}$ | $\frac{2}{36}$ | $\frac{3}{36}$ | $\frac{4}{36}$ | $\frac{5}{36}$ | $\frac{6}{36}$ | $\frac{5}{36}$ | $\frac{4}{36}$ | $\frac{3}{36}$ | $\frac{2}{36}$ | $\frac{1}{36}$ |

Until 1250, people believed that there were only 56 possible ways of throwing three dice. Richard de Fournival was the first to describe the accurate number of ways that three dice might fall.

### ▲ THREE DICE

*In how many ways can three dice be thrown?*

*The number of pips on three dice can add up to the totals of 3 through 18. Can you work out the probability of getting totals of 7 and 10 in a throw of three dice?*

*For centuries it was believed that there were only 56 possible ways of throwing three dice; people failed to recognize the difference between a set (combination) and a sequence (permutation). They counted sets only, when sequences should have been counted to get an accurate assessment of each roll's probability.*

*ANSWER: PAGE 109*

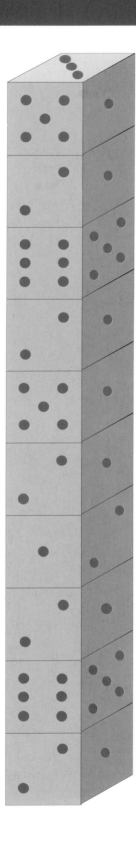

### ◀ DICE STACK

*Can you add up the number of dots on all the unseen sides?*

*The touching faces within the stack have identical numbers.*

ANSWER: PAGE 110

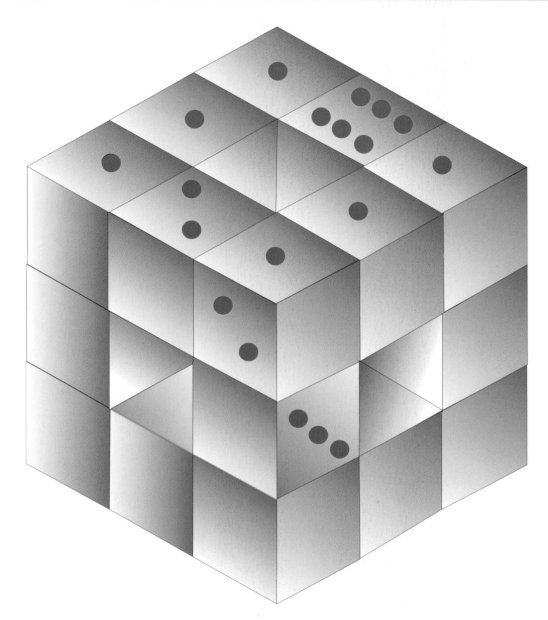

### ▲ DICE CUBE WITH HOLES

*A large cube was created by gluing together 20 standard dice. Die faces match wherever they are glued together, domino-style. In the middle of each side of the large cube there is a hole.*

*Can you first work out the numbers on the four sides of the dice forming the three visible holes in the big cube?*

*Can you then also work out the numbers on the three holes which are hidden?*

ANSWER: PAGE 110

### ▼ ICOSAHEDRAL DIE GAME

*There are two containers. Twenty numbered disks start out in the left-hand container, while the right container is empty. An icosahedral (20-sided) die is thrown by one of the players and the disk with the corresponding number is transferred from one container to the other. The graph shows the number of disks in the left-hand container after each of 100 throws of the die. After every 10 throws the containers are checked and the winner is the player whose container contains more disks than the other.*

*What happens in this game and, in the long run, which player is likely to win more often?*

ANSWER: PAGE 110

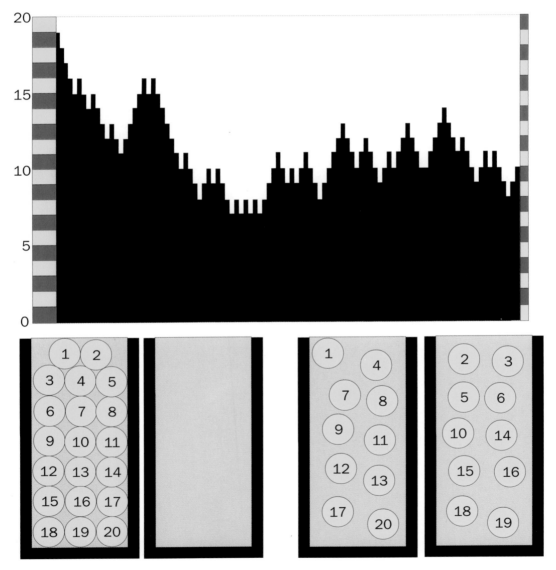

Start of the game

The state of the containers after
100 throws of the icosahedral die

Prime numbers provide the inspiration for many mathematical problems and puzzles.

## 2   3   4   5   6   7

## 8   9   10   11   12   13   14

## 15   16   17   18   19   20   21   ...

### ▲ PRIME DOUBLES

*Can you always find a prime number somewhere between any number and its double?*

ANSWER: PAGE 110

## ▼ GEMS

*A special stand was designed for the exhibition of the most famous gems in the world. The final selection included seven gems. How can the stand, which now accommodates only six gems, also include the seventh in just as prominent a position as the rest?*

ANSWER: PAGE 111

Coin tossing reveals many principles of probability. It also allows us to devise a number of brain-teasing puzzles for you to solve. Read on and then try the puzzles on the following pages.

## ❋ Coin tossing

One of the earliest paradoxes of probability is the one called "The Paradox of D'Alembert": When tossing two coins there are three possible outcomes. Is the chance for each of these outcomes 1 out of 3? In truth, these results are not equally likely, a fact which escaped the attention of D'Alembert and many others in his time.

There are four possible results when tossing two coins (or two tosses of a single coin), which an average person today is quite well aware of! A lucky guy travelling back in time with this bit of knowledge could easily become a very lucky gambler indeed.

Numbering or coloring the two coins helps to show that there are, in fact, four possible results:

1) Heads 1, Heads 2
2) Tails 1, Tails 2
3) Heads 1, Tails 2
4) Tails 1, Heads 2

Consequently, the probability of a toss of heads and tails occuring (2:4 = 1:2) is twice as high as that of either of the other two combinations (both 1:4).

When a coin is tossed into the air no one can say which way it will land. Yet toss that coin a million times and it will, with increasingly minor variations, come up heads half the time and tails the rest. In essence, this is the basis of the theory of probability.

Basically, two laws underlie probability, a "both-and" law, to calculate the probability of two events both happening, and an "either-or" law, to calculate the probability of one or the other of two events happening. The both-and law states that the chance of two independent events both happening is equal to the probability of one happening multiplied by the probability of the other event happening.

For instance, the chance of one flip of a coin coming up heads is $1/2$. The chance of heads landing face up on both the first and second flip is $1/2 \times 1/2$ or only $1/4$. The either-or law states that the chance of one or the other of two mutually exclusive probabilities coming true equals the sum of the separate chance of each coming true individually. For instance, the chance of turning up either heads or tails on a flip of a coin is equal to the chance of throwing heads plus the chance of throwing tails: $1/2 + 1/2 = 1$.

But what is the situation when tossing three coins or more?

Pascal's famous triangle gives us all the answers for any number of tosses. In Pascal's triangle, the first number in a line is the number of ways that number of coins can all come up heads; the next number is the number of ways all the coins but one can come up heads, and so on...For example: When tossing four coins, the probability of tossing all heads is $1/16$. Looking at Pascal's triangle (on page 10), can you determine the probability of tossing five heads in a set of 10 tossed coins?

First determine how many different ways such a throw can happen. The intersection of diagonal 5 and row 10 provides the answer: 252. Now add the numbers in the 10th row to obtain the number of possible throws. This is a short cut; the sum of the nth row is always $2^n$. The probability of getting five heads is $252/1024$.

Heads

Ta ils

▲ **COIN TOSSING**

*The lady is tossing a coin five times in a row.*
*How many different outcomes are possible?*

ANSWER: PAGE 111

Tossing three coins should result in at least two of the coins coming up alike, but what are the chances that the third one will do the same?

### ▲ FLIPPING THREE COINS

*What are the chances of three coins turning up alike—that is, either all heads or all tails?*

*Will the following reasoning provide the right answer?*

*When flipping three coins, at least two of the coins must come up alike. Since there is an even chance for a third coin to turn up heads or tails, the chance of all three coins turning up alike should be 1 in 2…or should it?*

Answer: page 111

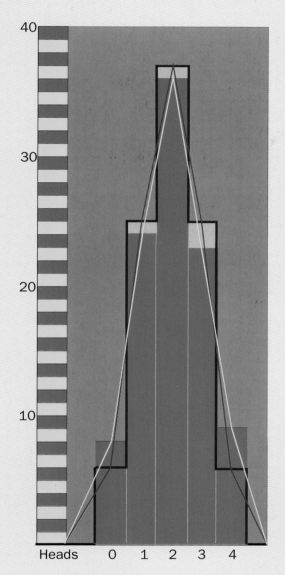

Heads   0   1   2   3   4

Red graph: statistical result

Blue outline: Probability
according to Pascal's triangle

### ▼ FOUR-COIN TOSS

*These are the results of a statistical experiment in which four coins were tossed 100 times. The number of heads appearing in each toss was recorded, creating a frequency graph of the outcomes, which can be compared to a graph of the outcomes according to the laws of probability.*

*If we had increased the number of tosses, the outcome would have more closely approached the theoretical curve, but even so, there is a good approximation of the probabilities from the fourth row of Pascal's triangle.*

*Try your own experiment.*

| | | | | | | | | | |
|---|---|---|---|---|---|---|---|---|---|
| 2 | 1 | 3 | 1 | 1 | 2 | 2 | 2 | 1 | 1 |
| 1 | 0 | 4 | 2 | 2 | 2 | 2 | 1 | 2 | 1 |
| 1 | 2 | 3 | 2 | 2 | 4 | 3 | 0 | 2 | 1 |
| 2 | 2 | 1 | 1 | 0 | 2 | 0 | 2 | 1 | 2 |
| 1 | 1 | 1 | 3 | 2 | 2 | 1 | 2 | 2 | 2 |
| 2 | 3 | 2 | 4 | 2 | 2 | 0 | 1 | 3 | 2 |
| 1 | 1 | 0 | 3 | 3 | 2 | 3 | 3 | 3 | 2 |
| 1 | 1 | 1 | 1 | 0 | 4 | 0 | 4 | 4 | 2 |
| 3 | 4 | 3 | 4 | 2 | 3 | 2 | 3 | 3 | 2 |
| 3 | 4 | 3 | 3 | 3 | 3 | 3 | 3 | 2 | 2 |

My experiment

| Number of Heads | Tally | Frequency | Pascal |
|---|---|---|---|
| 0 | 8 | 8 % | 6 % |
| 1 | 24 | 24 % | 25% |
| 2 | 36 | 36 % | 37% |
| 3 | 23 | 23 % | 25% |
| 4 | 9 | 9 % | 6 % |

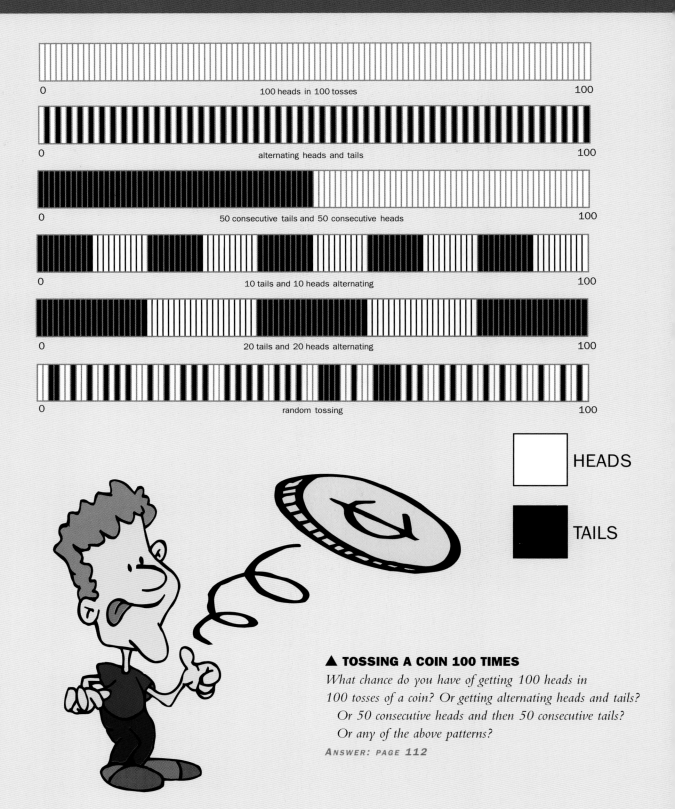

0    100 heads in 100 tosses    100

0    alternating heads and tails    100

0    50 consecutive tails and 50 consecutive heads    100

0    10 tails and 10 heads alternating    100

0    20 tails and 20 heads alternating    100

0    random tossing    100

HEADS

TAILS

### ▲ TOSSING A COIN 100 TIMES

*What chance do you have of getting 100 heads in 100 tosses of a coin? Or getting alternating heads and tails? Or 50 consecutive heads and then 50 consecutive tails? Or any of the above patterns?*

ANSWER: PAGE 112

## ▼ MÖBIUS GRAPH EDGE COLORING

*A ten-point graph is embedded in a Möbius band as shown.*

*How many colors are required to color the edges between the points of the graph so that no two edges of the same color meet at any point? (Straight lines that cross at an intersection not marked with a circle may be the same or different colors.)*

ANSWER: PAGE 112

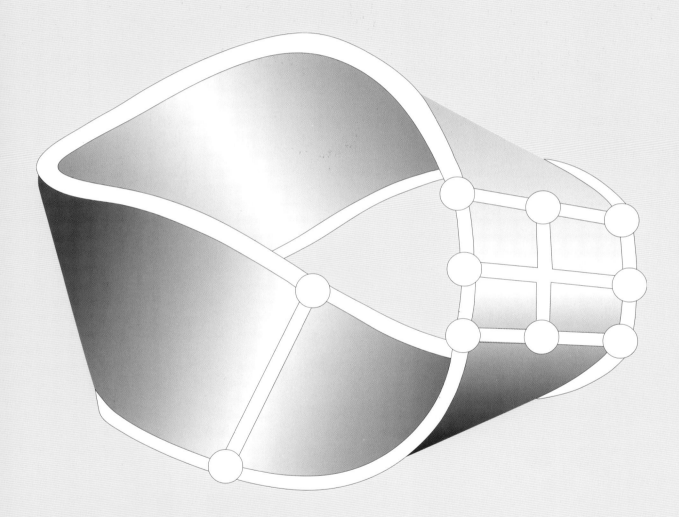

### ▼ IMAGINATION: A GAME FOR TWO PLAYERS

*Players imagine a vertical mirror which can be placed on one of the colored and numbered lines on each of the cards. One player choses red while the other takes blue as his or her color.*

*Players take turns placing their imaginary mirror on one of the lines on each of the 18 cards, the objective being to count the greatest possible number of beads in their color, while counting the least possible number of beads of the opponent's color. A player may not use the same line as their opponent. All the reflected beads are counted in the score which is calculated as the difference in number between one player's color and his or her opponents color. See the answer page for extra blank score cards.*

*Can you find the best scores for both red and blue on each of the 18 cards?*

ANSWER: PAGES *112–113*

| Card number | BLUE | | RED | |
|:---:|:---:|:---:|:---:|:---:|
| | line | score | line | score |
| 1 | | | | |
| 2 | | | | |
| 3 | | | | |
| 4 | | | | |
| 5 | | | | |
| 6 | | | | |
| 7 | | | | |
| 8 | | | | |
| 9 | | | | |
| 10 | | | | |
| 11 | | | | |
| 12 | | | | |
| 13 | | | | |
| 14 | | | | |
| 15 | | | | |
| 16 | | | | |
| 17 | | | | |
| 18 | | | | |
| Total | | | | |

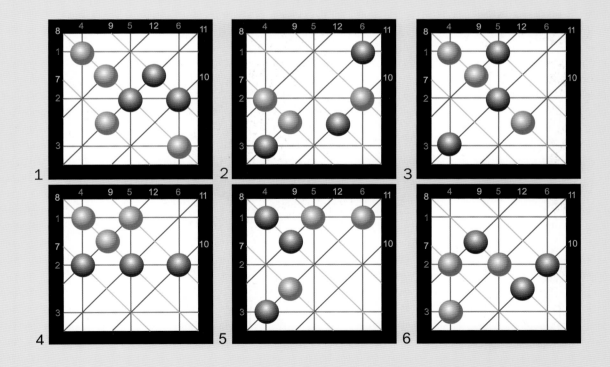

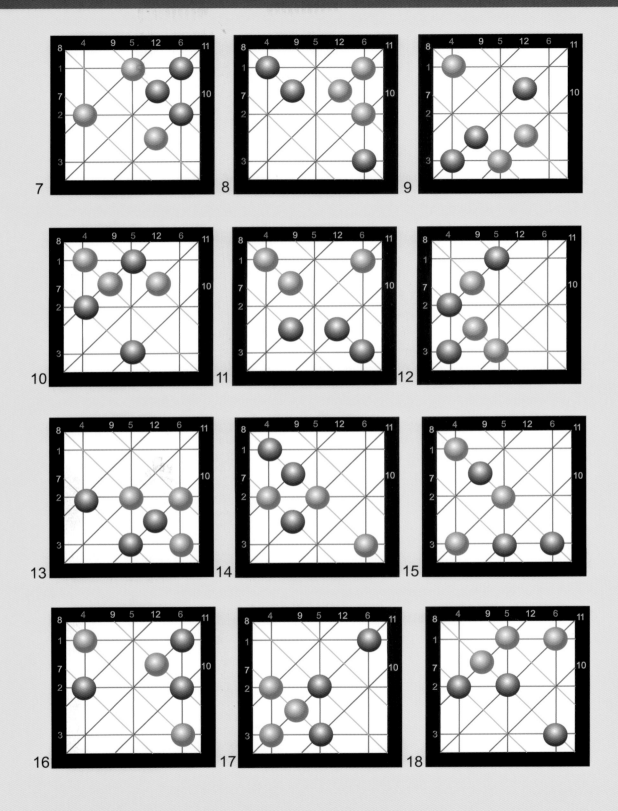

Probability theory is one of science's most useful mathematical tools. It makes possible the prediction of the whole from a limited sample and allows scientists to make estimates of reliability and error.

"*From a purely operational point of view...the concept of randomness is so elusive as to cease to be viable.*"
*Mark Kac, mathematician*

▶ **PROBABILITY MACHINE**

*In the probability machine on the right, the red balls on top are released when the yellow gate is opened. At each obstacle each falling ball has two possibilities: to go left or right.*

*The numbers on the obstacles indicate the number of paths leading to them. The pattern these numbers form is the famous Pascal's triangle.*

*If a great number of balls is released and the experiment is repeated many times, then the number of balls falling into each lower compartment will, on average, form a direct correlation with the ratio of the number of paths leading to that compartment. On the other hand, the path of one specific ball among the many will be completely random and unpredictable.*

*In our machine, we are releasing 64 balls from the top. How many, on the average, will end up in each of the seven compartments below, according to the laws of probability?*

ANSWER: PAGE 114

## ✳ **Probability machine**

Our probability machine is a simplified design version of the classical machine, or "Galton board," first constructed by Francis Galton in the 19th century. The device demonstrated how a probability curve can be found by experiment.

It is indeed a strikingly beautiful and effective science experiment—that of visually observing the effect of completely random actions of the bouncing balls, which ultimately form nearly the same predictable curve each time the experiment is repeated.

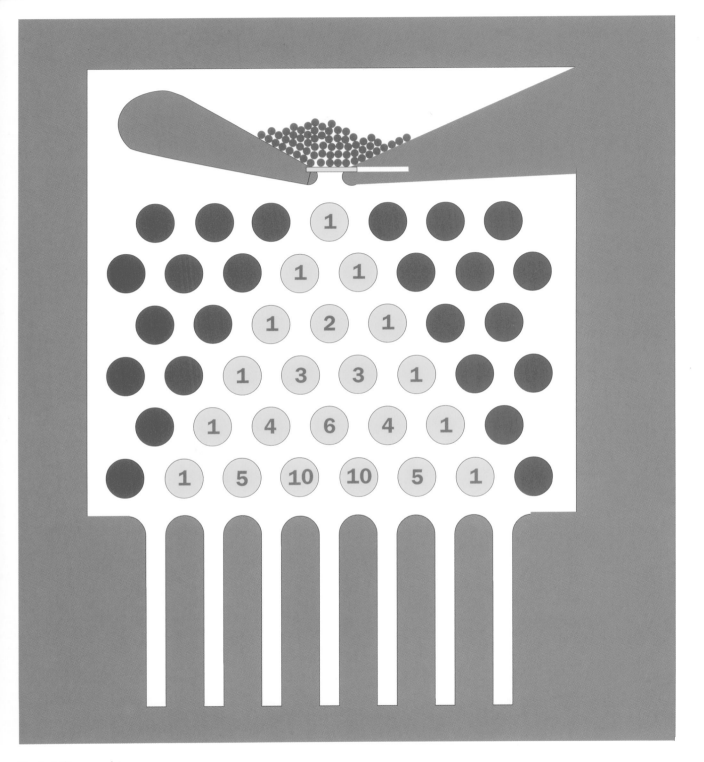

Probability machine

Probability machine

## ▲ PREDICTABLE AND UNPREDICTABLE EVENTS

*Study the two simple physics demonstration devices shown here. In both, steel balls are released at the top and land in compartments below.*

*In the first, called a "probability machine," the released steel balls collide with an array of regularly spaced disks before they fall into compartments below.*

*In the other device, called a "free-fall machine," the released* *balls fall on a steel platform (which can be adjusted at any desired angle) and are reflected before they land in one of the compartments below.*

*Can you predict into which compartment a single steel ball will fall, and what the trajectories of the balls will be in each device?*

ANSWER: PAGE 115

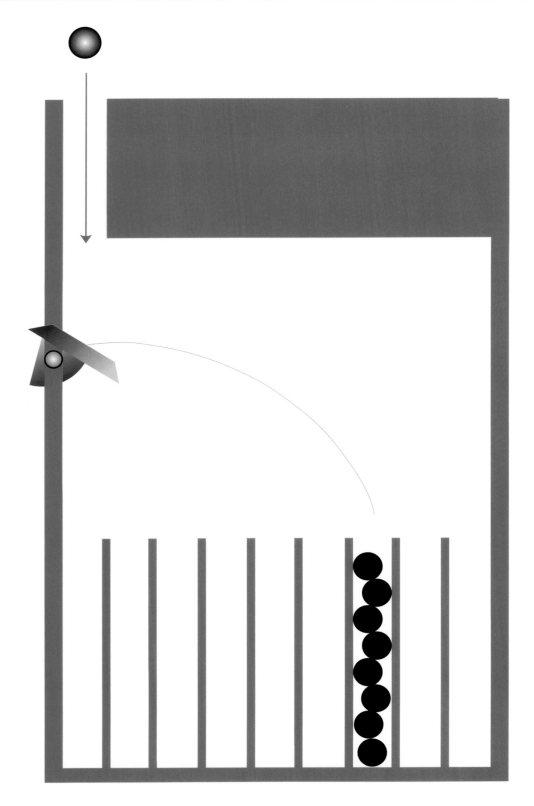

Free-fall
machine

### ▲ FOUR HATS GAME

*One should be cautious with statistical data and percentages when two or more groups are combined to form a single group.*

*It's a common belief that the larger the data set, the more reliable one can expect one's conclusion to be. Simpson's paradox deals a heavy blow to this assumption. Sometimes results from a large data set are, in fact, misleading.*

*The four hats game will demonstrate such a paradox.*

*Puzzle 1) Precisely 41 chips are distributed in four hats on the big table, 23 red and 18 blue. The distribution of the chips can be seen in the illustration.*

*Draw one chip from each pair of hats (A and B, and then C and D). If you draw a red chip on either occasion you win. Which color hat in each pair are you likely to draw from to get a red chip?*

*Puzzle 2)* The same game is played again on the small table, by placing the chips from the two red hats into one red hat and similarly consolidating the contents of the blue hats.

From which hat do you now have to choose in order to have your best chance of drawing a red chip?

ANSWER: PAGE 115

## ▼ DROWNING IN THE LAKE

*Did you hear about poor Ernie, the 5-foot-tall boy who couldn't swim and drowned in a shallow lake whose average depth was 3 feet?*

*How could this unfortunate accident happen?*

ANSWER: PAGE 116

## ▼ THE PROBLEM OF X

The following problem shows the importance of precise meaning where averages and probabilities are involved.

If you know nothing about x, except that it lies somewhere between 9 and 11 on the ruler, what would your best guess be as to the value of x in order to minimize the possible percentage error (that is, the difference between your guess and the actual value of x, expressed as a percentage of x)?

ANSWER: PAGE 116

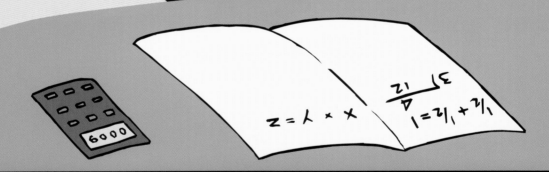

### ▲ PREDICTING EARTHQUAKES

*Madam "X" has correctly predicted every major earthquake in California for the past year.*

*How did she do it?*

ANSWER: PAGE 116

## ▲ LOOK IN THE TUBE

*From which direction do you see the person through the tube—left or right?*

ANSWER: PAGE 116

### ▲ TRIPLE DUEL

*Tom, Bill, and Mike decide to settle their differences by first drawing straws to determine the order in which they will shoot. Each will then take one shot at the target of their choice until only one is standing.*

*Tom and Bill are dead shots and never miss, while Mike is only average and has a 50% success rate.*

*Who has the best chance of survival?*

ANSWER: PAGE 117

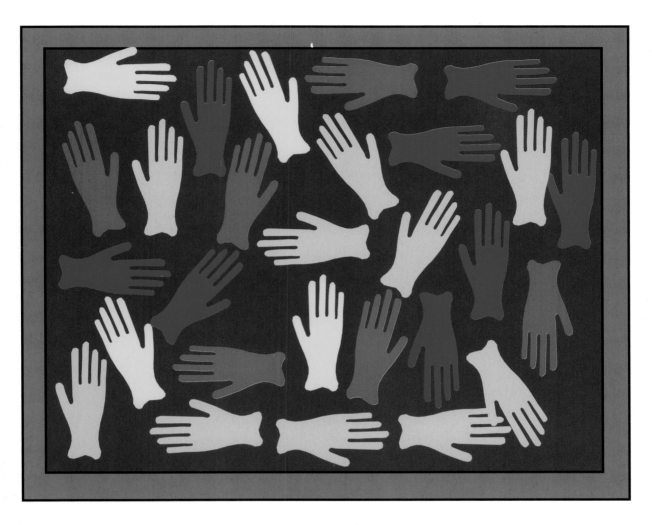

2 pairs

3 pairs

4 pairs

5 pairs

### ▲ GLOVES IN THE DARK

*In the drawer I have two pairs of yellow gloves, three pairs of red gloves, four pairs of green gloves, and five pairs of blue gloves.*

*In complete darkness, how many gloves do I have to chose to ensure having a complete pair of gloves in one of the colors and with proper handedness?*

ANSWER: PAGE 120

Like the previous puzzle, we will assume that you never pair your socks before putting them away in a drawer. Try this puzzle in an attempt to get a matching pair.

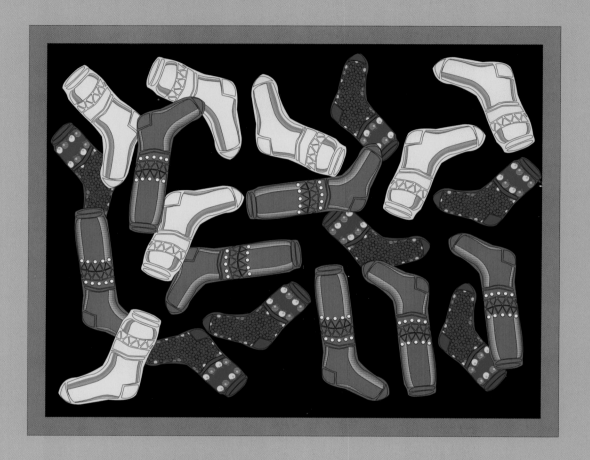

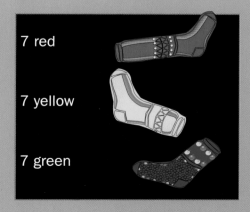

7 red

7 yellow

7 green

### ▲ SOCKS IN THE DARK

*In the drawer I have seven red, seven yellow, and seven green socks.*

*In complete darkness, how many socks must I draw to get a matching pair of any color?*

*And how many must I draw to have a pair of each color?*

ANSWER: PAGE 121

### ▲ LOST SOCKS

*Imagine you have ten pairs of socks and two socks are lost. What is more likely:*

*1) The best possible scenario—the two lost socks constitute one complete pair, and you are left with nine complete pairs?; or*

*2) The worst possible scenario—the two socks are single socks, in which case you are left with only eight complete pairs and two single socks?*

*How much more likely is one than the other?*

ANSWER: PAGE 121

The brain tricks the eye into seeing what isn't there in the case of these illusions. Both require you to focus on the illustrations in a particular way, however, in order to glimpse what you are intended to see.

### ▲ REVOLVING CIRCLES

*This is a composition inspired by the "video-active" paintings of the Parisian artist Isia Leviant.*

*If you stare for long enough at the colored concentric circles you will see the illusion of a white blur appearing on the circles and revolving at a high speed.*

## ▼ NEON SPREADING ILLUSION

*You can see that in the matrix below red crosses replace some grid crossings, and blue crosses replace others. The red and blue appear to spread diagonally.*

   *This illusion was discovered in 1984 by Christoph Redies, Lothar Spillman, and Prispian Kuuz. What happens if you rotate the page 45 degrees?*

ANSWER: PAGE 121

The properties of a shape can be fascinating and will make you see everyday objects in new ways.

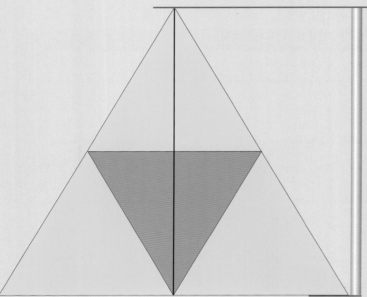

## ▲ BROKEN STICK

*If a walking stick is broken at random into three pieces, what is the probability that the pieces can be put together in a triangle?*

*The equilateral triangle shown will be helpful in solving this classic probability problem. Its height is equal to the length of the stick.*

ANSWER: PAGE 122

"**B**esides learning to see. there is another art to be learned—not to see what is not."
*Maria Mitchell, astronomer*

## ▲ PRIVATE EYE

*Can the private eye see the burglar?*

ANSWER: PAGE 122

**S**ome people take a walk when they need to think about a problem. Let's hope these puzzles don't have you travelling around in circles.

**N**othing in Nature is random. A thing appears random only through the incompleteness of our knowledge.
*Spinoza*

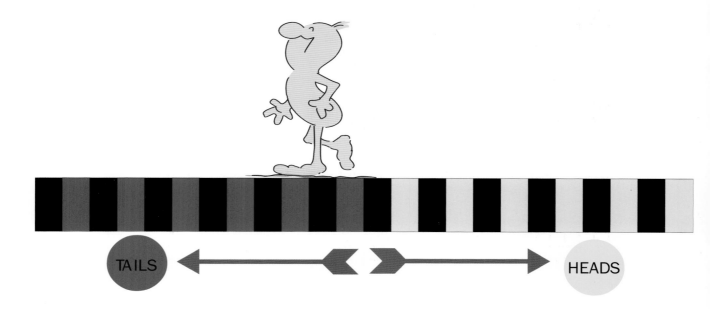

### ▲ RANDOM WALK

*For this puzzle, flip a coin repeatedly.*

*If it comes down heads, the walker will move one mark to the right; if tails he will move one mark to the left.*

*After many flips of the coin, let's say 36 flips, can you guess how far from his starting point our walker will be?*

*After your guess, flip the coin 36 times to check your prediction.*

*Can you also tell what the chances are that our walker will return to his starting point at some point in his walk? (Assume that the walk continues indefinitely.)*

*ANSWER: PAGE 123*

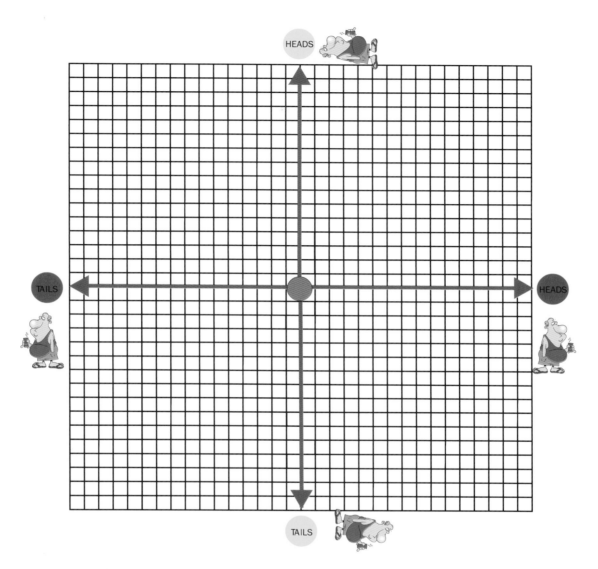

## ▲ RANDOM DRUNKARD'S WALK

In the drunkard's random walk, starting from the central lamppost, moves are dictated by flipping two coins at the same time (a red and yellow coin). On each flip on the two coins, the drunkard walks one square north or south (based on the yellow coin's outcome) and one square east or west (based on the red coin's outcome).

This is the simplest demonstration of a stochastic (which means "random") process, and a good analogy for explaining Brownian motion, in which a particle is "kicked around" by molecules of a surrounding liquid or gas.

Where do you think the drunkard will be after 100 flips of the two coins?

Can you also guess what the chances are that the drunkard will return to his starting point at the lamppost at some point?

Consider the walk as finite by treating the side of the grid as a barrier. At the edge, ignore any flips that would take the drunkard off the grid, but continue moving him when it is possible to do so.

ANSWER: PAGE 123

## WHO TELLS THE TRUTH?

*On these two pages we shall meet members of the Trut and Fals families. Members of the Trut family always tell the truth, while members of the Fals family always lie.*

*To which family does each person belong?*

ANSWER: PAGE 124

Ever tried making your own set of nontransitive dice? Use our template to help you solve the puzzle and play the game.

## ❊ Nontransitive games

Most relationships are transitive, which is to say: if A is bigger than B, and B is bigger than C, then A must also be bigger than C. But some relationships may be not transitive. If A is the father of B, and B is the father of C, it is never true that A is the father of C.

The game "rock, scissors, paper" is nontransitive. In this game rock breaks scissors, and scissors cut paper, but rock does not defeat paper.

Ancient Chinese philosophers divided matter into five categories forming a nontransitive cycle: wood gives birth to fire, fire to earth, earth to metal, metal to water, water to wood and so on.

In probability theory there are relations which are seemingly transitive when they are actually not. These relationships are called nontransitive paradoxes or games.

A great deal of ingenuity can go into creating such paradoxes and games, which are perfect "sucker bets."

Some of the most astonishing examples of such games are nontransitive dice sets, like the set in our puzzle. Such dice were first designed by Bradley Efron at Stanford University, and were opened to wider audiences by Martin Gardner in his column.

### ▶ NONTRANSITIVE DICE

*Make a set of four dice as shown at right.*

*Ask a partner to choose one of the four dice; you then choose one of the remaining three. Taking turns, throw each die; the higher number wins.*

*Can you figure out how to choose the die which will allow you to win in the long run?*

ANSWER: PAGE 126

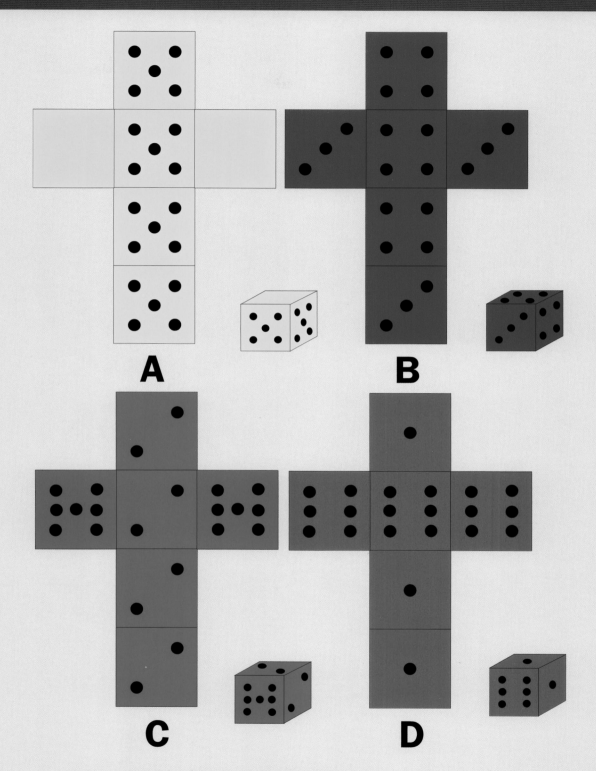

**A**

**B**

**C**

**D**

Cut-out models of the four nontransitive dice

No need to get in a spin about the puzzles on these pages. Use what you you've learnt about nontransitive relationships and the laws of probability.

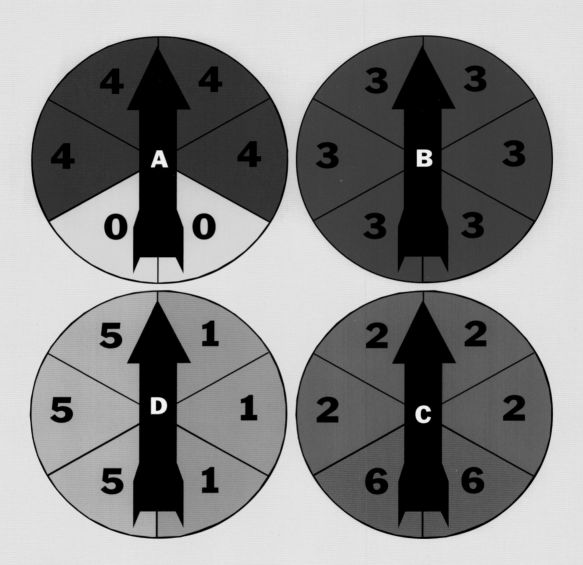

### ▲ NONTRANSITIVE SPINNERS 1

*Two players each choose a spinner and play a series of rounds by spinning their spinners; the higher number wins each round.*

*Can you work out the winning odds between any two spinners so that you have the advantage no matter what spinner your opponent chooses to use?*

ANSWER: PAGE 127

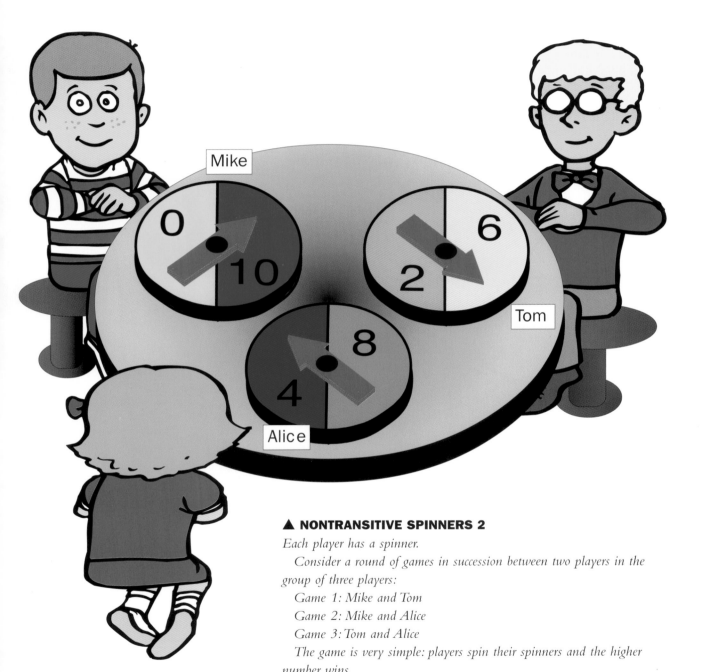

### ▲ NONTRANSITIVE SPINNERS 2

*Each player has a spinner.*

*Consider a round of games in succession between two players in the group of three players:*

*Game 1: Mike and Tom*

*Game 2: Mike and Alice*

*Game 3: Tom and Alice*

*The game is very simple: players spin their spinners and the higher number wins.*

*Which player is most likely to be the winner in the long run?*

ANSWER: PAGE *128*

### ▲ NONTRANSITIVE SPINNERS 3

*The game has three spinners. The first spinner (A) has only one value: 3. The second spinner (B) is more complex; just over half of it (56%) has a value of 2, and just under half (the remaining 44%) is equally divided between values of 4 and 6. The third spinner (C) is divided so that a tiny bit more than half of it (51%) is worth 1 and the rest (49%) is worth 5.*

*Players choose spinners and spin the arrows to see which spinner wins.*

*Which is likely to be the most successful spinner if there is to be a long series of one-on-one games? What about if all three players compete simultaneously?*

ANSWER: PAGE 128

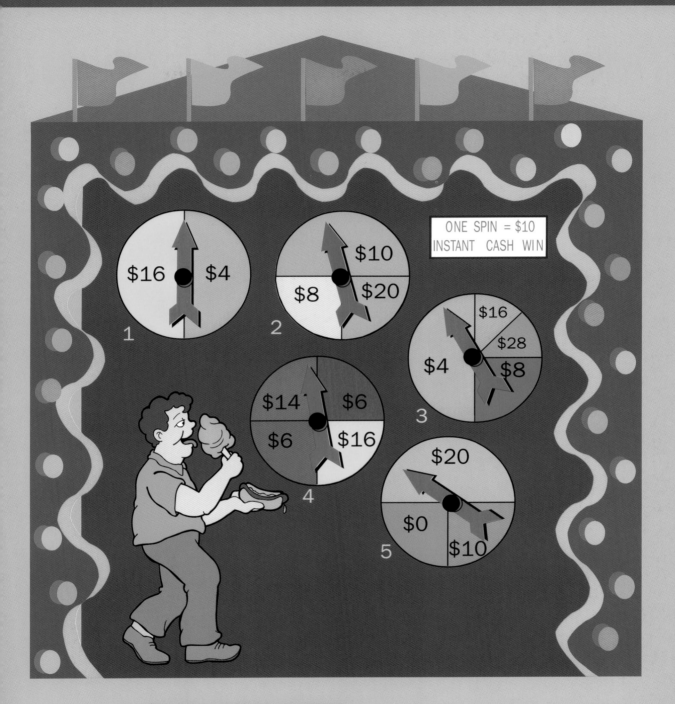

ONE SPIN = $10
INSTANT CASH WIN

▲ **LUCKY CARNIVAL SPINNERS**

*To play this game you pay $10 for a spin, choose the spinner of your*
*choice, spin, and win the amount spun.*

*Which spinner is your best choice?*

ANSWER: PAGE *128*

▶ **WATERMELONS (page 6)**

My intuitive guess was "about 800 pounds," far from the solution. I hope you did better.

The surprising and completely counterintuitive answer is 500 pounds, which is not difficult to work out once you take paper and pencil and make a simple calculation. See the graphs at right for further explanation.

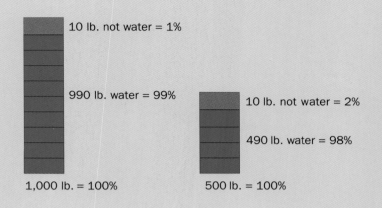

10 lb. not water = 1%

990 lb. water = 99%

1,000 lb. = 100%

10 lb. not water = 2%

490 lb. water = 98%

500 lb. = 100%

▼ **RAFFLE (page 7)**

There are 90 ways the couple can win and 30 ways they can lose.

The probability that they will not win is 30 in 120, or 1 in 4 (25%).

▼ **PASCAL'S TRIANGLE (page 10)**

Each number in Pascal's triangle is the sum of the two numbers above it to the left and right.

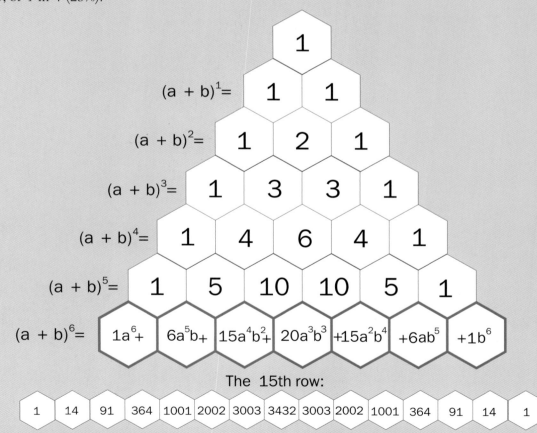

$(a + b)^1 =$

$(a + b)^2 =$

$(a + b)^3 =$

$(a + b)^4 =$

$(a + b)^5 =$

$(a + b)^6 =$ $1a^6 +$ $6a^5b +$ $15a^4b^2 +$ $20a^3b^3$ $+15a^2b^4$ $+6ab^5$ $+1b^6$

The 15th row:

| 1 | 14 | 91 | 364 | 1001 | 2002 | 3003 | 3432 | 3003 | 2002 | 1001 | 364 | 91 | 14 | 1 |

**HATS AND FIVE STICKERS (page 11)**

If B and C both had blue stickers on, A would know his sticker was red. But A doesn't know his color; therefore at least one, and possibly both, of hats B and C have a red sticker. If C had a blue sticker B would know he had a red sticker. But B doesn't know, so C must have a red sticker.

**GAMBLER'S DICE PROBLEMS (page 14)**

1) On any given roll of a die, the odds that the six will not come up are 5/6. Since each roll of a die is independent of the others, the chance of not rolling a six in a given series can be calculated as:

two rolls: $5/6 \times 5/6 = 0.69$

three rolls: $5/6 \times 5/6 \times 5/6 = 0.57$

four rolls: $5/6 \times 5/6 \times 5/6 \times 5/6 = 0.48$

which means that you have a 52% chance of rolling at least one six after four rolls.

2) The probability of rolling at least one double-six in 24 throws is the same as 1 minus the probability of rolling no double-sixes in 24 throws. This second calculation is easily worked out on a scientific calculator: 35/36 to the power of 24 is 0.51 approximately, so the player's odds of winning are $1 - 0.51 = 49\%$ approximately.

▶ **THROWING A DIE (page 15)**

The probability that both of you will throw the same number is 1 in 6. Therefore the probability that one of you will throw higher than the other is 5 in 6.

This is halved to give the probability that one of you will get a higher number than the other:

$15/36 = 5/12$.

The outcome table illustrates the probabilities:

| | 1 | 2 | 3 | 4 | 5 | 6 |
|---|---|---|---|---|---|---|
| 1 | * | + | + | + | + | + |
| 2 | - | * | + | + | + | + |
| 3 | - | - | * | + | + | + |
| 4 | - | - | - | * | + | + |
| 5 | - | - | - | - | * | + |
| 6 | - | - | - | - | - | + |

### ▼ FIGURE-GROUND (page 17)

What do you see in the pattern?

If you look at the figure long enough, you can alternately see a radially marked cross or a concentrically marked cross. One's impression of the crosses depends on whether they are classified as figure or ground. Take the green concentric circles; when they are part of the ground, they do not appear interrupted. On the contrary, one has the impression that the concentric circles continue behind the figure. Nothing of this kind is observed when the green areas are seen as figure.

The patterns can be organized in different ways, and we do this alternately. The eye cannot choose between them and is forced to repeatedly shift from one area to another. There is no rule as to what is perceived as figure. By a switch of attention to a different part of the pattern, or by sweeping the eyes to and fro across the field, you can see a succession of parts as figural, each one in turn.

### ▼ HOLLOW CUBE 1 (page 18)

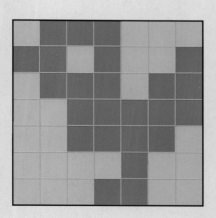

### ▼ HOLLOW CUBE 2 (page 19)

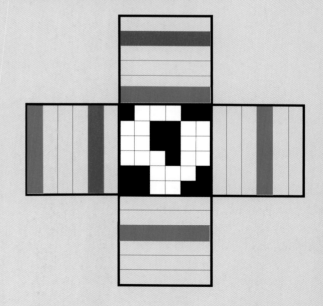

## ▶ MIXED HATS (page 21)

Puzzle 1) There are six possible ways for the three hats to be mixed as shown right.

In four of these, one of the men gets his own hat. Therefore the probability of at least one man getting his own hat is 4 in 6, or 0.66—a good bet.

Puzzle 2) The number of ways that n hats can be permuted is n!, in our case 6! = 720 (6! = 6 × 5 × 4 × 3 × 2 × 1 = 720. How many of these permutations give each man a wrong hat?

A simple method of finding this number involves the transcendental number e = 2.718. . . .

The number of all wrong permutations of n objects is the number that is closest to n! divided by e.

In our case 720/2.718 = 265; thus the probability that no man gets back his own hat is 265/720 = 0.368055.

Subtracting this result from 1 (certainty) we obtain 0.6321, the probability of at least one man getting back his own hat.

## CORNER CUBE (page 22)

The corner cube is one of the classical alternating perspective figures. Some two-dimensional figures can be interpreted in more than one way in three dimensions. The corner cube can be interpreted in three ways. The perception of any of these won't last for too long.

## INTERRUPTIONS (page 23)

The message is MASTERMIND.

You can read it when looking at the page from below at a slanted angle.

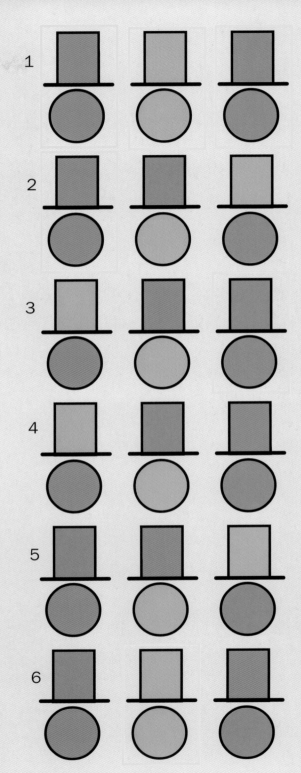

1

2

3

4

5

6

▶ **ROLLING CUBE (page 24)**

The smallest board you can use to get a different orientation of a cube on each square is the 4-by-6 board as shown.

The path of the rolling cube is shown by the arrows.

▼ **ROLLING DICE (page 25)**

Puzzle 1)

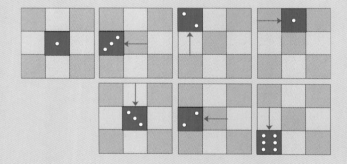

Puzzle 2) From the starting position you can roll the die so that it can end on any square with any face on top.

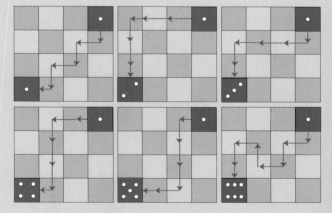

## LOADED DICE (page 37)

By dropping the dice carefully into a glass of water.

A loaded die will tend to turn while descending, while a fair die will sink to the bottom in the same orientation without rotating. Professional pit bosses in casinos can use a special pair of callipers to balance the die across different corners.

## ROTATING WINDOW (page 40)

If the window is rotated at a slow constant speed, we will, surprisingly enough, see it as an oscillating rectangle and not as a rotating trapezoid.

When you stick a pencil through one of the window holes, even more surprising things will occur. Some people will see the pencil go through different actions—it will seem to bend or twist and its speed and shape will vary as it turns.

The painted shadows cause an even more complex series of illusions.

Any small object attached to the rotating window (like the bird on page 40) will seem to move in the opposite direction to the window.

## MATH PANEL (page 41)

There are 7! ways to arrange all 7 people = 5040.

There are five ways all the bearded people could sit together:

B B B X X X X
X B B B X X X
X X B B B X X
X X X B B B X
X X X X B B B

For each of these five arrangements, the bearded people have $3 \times 2 \times 1 = 6$ ways of arranging themselves. Also, the non-bearded people have $4 \times 3 \times 2 \times 1 = 24$ ways that they could sit in each of the five arrangements. Therefore, there are $5 \times 6 \times 24 = 720$ ways in which the bearded people can sit next to each other.

The probability of this happening is therefore 1 in 7 (720/5040).

## TWO FAMILIES (page 42)

This is the sort of problem for which Pascal's triangle (see page 10) will easily provide the answer. The eighth row of Pascal's triangle gives us the probability of getting four children of each sex: 70/256, or about 27%.

The probability of getting eight children of the same sex is 1/256, or less than 1%. It may be that more than only chance is involved when families have six or more children of the same sex, which occurs twice as often as chance says it should. It seems that genetic factors may come into play.

Note that having four girls and four boys is more likely because the order of birth doesn't matter. Any specific arrangement of four boys and four girls, such as GBBGGBGB, would be exactly as likely as GGGGGGGG or BBBBBBBB.

## TWO-CHILD FAMILIES (page 43)

This problem was posed in Marilyn Vos Savant's column in *Parade* magazine. Her answer was that the probability of the woman having two boys was about 33%, whereas the probability that the man had two boys was 50%.

For the woman with at least one boy there are three possibilities:

| Older child | B | G | B |
|---|---|---|---|
| Younger child | G | B | B |

Each of these possibilities is equally likely, so the probability that she has two boys is 1 in 3, about 33%.

For the man there are only two possibilites:

| Older child | B | B |
|---|---|---|
| Younger child | G | B |

With two equally likely possibilities, the probability is 50%.

## BEST CANDIDATE (page 45)

Interviewing 36 candidates before selecting the next candidate to improve upon the first 36 will improve your chances to 1 in 3, and this is the best you can do.

Another option would be to compromise, and decide that it would also be acceptable to hire the second best candidate.

With such a compromise, by lowering the sample group to 30 candidates you will have a better than 50% chance of choosing the best or the second best. Or, if you can be satisfied by hiring any of the five best and take a sample group of 20, you will have a 70% of choosing one of the top five candidates for the job.

## THROWING A SIX (page 46)

Obviously, the probability is not 100%.

In fact, you have to calculate the probability of *not* throwing a six, six times in a row.

The probability of not throwing a six on any throw is 5/6.

$5/6 \times 5/6 \times 5/6 \times 5/6 \times 5/6 \times 5/6 = 0.33$

Therefore, the probability of throwing a six over the course of six throws is high: $1 - 0.33 = 0.67$ or 67%.

## SIX TOSSES (page 47)

$6/6 \times 5/6 \times 4/6 \times 3/6 \times 2/6 \times 1/6 = 0.015$

… or less than a 2% chance.

## ROTATING SPIRAL (page 48)

When you stare at a moving pattern, your eyes and brain get used to seeing movement. When you look at something that's standing still, your eyes see movement in the opposite direction. The common name for this illusion is the waterfall effect.

If you stare at the revolving spiral for some time and then look at the still picture of the ship, it will suddenly seem to move toward you or away from you depending on the direction of the rotating spiral.

## RELIEFS OR CAVITIES (page 49)

When you turn the page upside down, reliefs change into cavities and cavities change into refliefs.

But when you stare at the shapes imagining that the light comes from below, you can reverse them without even turning the page upside down.

## PAIR OF DICE (page 50)

Puzzle 1) Leibniz was wrong. A total of 12 can occur in only one way (red die = 6 and blue die = 6), whereas a total of 11 can occur in two ways (red die = 6 and blue die = 5, or red die = 5 and blue die = 6). Thus their probabilities are different: 1/36 and 2/36 respectively, as you can easily read from the table.
Puzzle 2) With a pair of dice you can't roll a 1. There are six possible even numbers: 2, 4, 6, 8, 10, and 12. There are five odd numbers: 3, 5, 7, 9, and 11. There are 18 ways of rolling an even number, and 18 ways of rolling an odd one, as shown in the table. So the chances are even.

## THREE DICE (page 52)

The sums from 3 through 18 can come up in $6 \times 6 \times 6 = 216$ different ways when throwing three dice.

Seven can come up in 15 different ways (7%), while 10 can come up in 27 ways (12.5%).

### DICE STACK (page 53)

The sum of unseen faces is 155. One way to calculate this is to count all the visible spots and subtract from (21 spots × 10 dice) = 210.

### DICE CUBE WITH HOLES (page 54)

Visible holes:
Top:   4 – 2 – 3 – 6
Left:  5 – 4 – 1 – 3
Right: 6 – 2 – 1 – 2
Hidden holes:
Bottom: 3 – 5 – 3 – 2
Left:  5 – 6 – 1 – 2
Right: 3 – 1 – 3 – 6

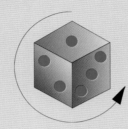

One should remember that all modern dice are left handed.

### ICOSAHEDRAL DIE GAME (page 55)

The disks will tend to flow from the left container to the right one until an equilibrium is reached (half of the disks in each container), after which the fluctations are not great.

   So the player with the left-hand container will tend to win the first few games, and maintain that lead as the disks even out.

   But complex calculations show that if the game is played long enough, all the disks will eventually wind up back in the left container, though this would take a very long time.

### PRIME DOUBLES (page 56)

There is always a prime between any integer greater than 1 and the integer's double.

## ▼ GEMS (page 57)

Simply turn the stand upside-down and arrange the seven gems as shown.

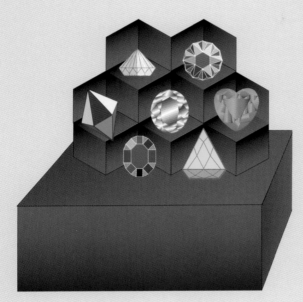

## COIN TOSSING (page 58–59)

Every time the coin is tossed there are two possible outcomes. We can conclude from the basic counting law below that the total number of possible outcomes is: $2 \times 2 \times 2 \times 2 \times 2 = 2^5 = 32$

Basic counting law:
If there are M possible ways a task can be performed and, after the first task is completed, there are N possible ways a second task can be performed, then there are M × N possible ways for the two tasks to be performed in order.

## FLIPPING THREE COINS (page 60)

The reasoning is incorrect. We already know that there are two different outcomes for flipping a single coin. We have also seen that there are four different outcomes for flipping two coins. We can show that there are eight different ways for three coins to turn up:

   HHH
   HHT
   HTH
   HTT
   THH
   THT
   TTH
   TTT

We can see that in only two of the eight cases are all three coins the same. Therefore, the correct probability is 2/8, or 1/4.

### TOSSING A COIN 100 TIMES (page 62)

To get 100 heads in 100 tosses of a coin:

1 head: $1/2 = 0.50$

2 heads: $1/2 \times 1/2 = 1/4 = 0.25$

3 heads: $1/2 \times 1/2 \times 1/2 = 1/8 = 0.125$

100 heads: $(1/2)^{100}$ = approximately $1/1,000,000,000,000,000,000,000,000,000,000$

It is theoretically possible to get 100 heads in 100 tosses of a coin, but it is mind-bogglingly unlikely because there are so many different configurations of mixed heads and tails.

Still, for the same reason, it is equally unlikely that you will get any other specific sequence. All the sequences shown have equally the same likelihood of occurring.

### ▼ MÖBIUS GRAPH EDGE COLORING (page 63)

It is impossible to color the graph using only three colors.

A fourth color is needed as shown.

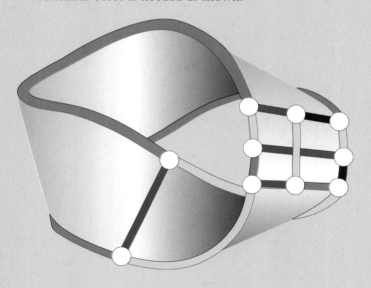

### ▼ IMAGINATION (page 64)

The chart shows the best scores for both red and blue on each of the 18 cards.

| Card number | BLUE | | RED | |
|:---:|:---:|:---:|:---:|:---:|
| | line | score | line | score |
| 1 | 2 | 3 | 8 | 3 |
| 2 | 12 | 1 | 1 | 1 |
| 3 | 7 | 2 | 7 | 2 |
| 4 | 12 | 3 | 2 | 3 |
| 5 | 5 | 3 | 5 | 3 |
| 6 | 7 | 3 | 7 | 3 |
| 7 | 5 | 3 | 5 | 3 |
| 8 | 5 | 4 | 5 | 4 |
| 9 | 10 | 2 | 12 | 2 |
| 10 | 2 | 3 | 2 | 3 |
| 11 | 2 | 6 | 2 | 6 |
| 12 | 11 | 2 | 4 | 2 |
| 13 | 8 | 3 | 8 | 3 |
| 14 | 5 | 3 | 5 | 3 |
| 15 | 10 | 3 | 10 | 3 |
| 16 | 9 | 2 | 9 | 2 |
| 17 | 5 | 4 | 5 | 4 |
| 18 | 2 | 4 | 2 | 4 |

▼ IMAGINATION SCORE CARDS (pages 64-65)

| Card number | BLUE | | RED | |
| --- | --- | --- | --- | --- |
| | line | score | line | score |
| 1 | | | | |
| 2 | | | | |
| 3 | | | | |
| 4 | | | | |
| 5 | | | | |
| 6 | | | | |
| 7 | | | | |
| 8 | | | | |
| 9 | | | | |
| 10 | | | | |
| 11 | | | | |
| 12 | | | | |
| 13 | | | | |
| 14 | | | | |
| 15 | | | | |
| 16 | | | | |
| 17 | | | | |
| 18 | | | | |
| Total | | | | |

| Card number | BLUE | | RED | |
| --- | --- | --- | --- | --- |
| | line | score | line | score |
| 1 | | | | |
| 2 | | | | |
| 3 | | | | |
| 4 | | | | |
| 5 | | | | |
| 6 | | | | |
| 7 | | | | |
| 8 | | | | |
| 9 | | | | |
| 10 | | | | |
| 11 | | | | |
| 12 | | | | |
| 13 | | | | |
| 14 | | | | |
| 15 | | | | |
| 16 | | | | |
| 17 | | | | |
| 18 | | | | |
| Total | | | | |

## ▼ PROBABILITY MACHINE (page 66)

The seven compartments correspond to the sixth row of Pascal's triangle: 1, 6, 15, 20, 15, 6, 1—the sum of which is 64, equalling the number of balls released in our experiment.

This outcome forms a crude approximation of the famous "Gauss curve," also known as the "IQ curve," "normal curve," "bell curve," or just as the probability curve, which plays an enormously important role in modern science.

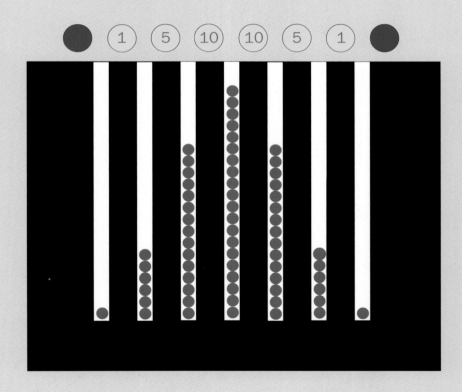

**PREDICTABLE AND UNPREDICTABLE EVENTS (pages 68–69)**

The two devices, respectively, demonstrate random and predictable events.
Puzzle 1) In the probability machine you can't predict the course of a
single ball, which falls in a random unpredictable pattern—yet you can
predict the average outcome of a great number of such single random
events, as the result of laws of chance, or probability. This outcome is
visualised by the Gaussian curve.

Puzzle 2) In the free-fall machine, on the other hand, once the steel
platform is fixed at a certain angle, the falling ball moves on a predictable
path according to the laws of physics—in a path which is a parabola—and
will always land in the same compartment at the bottom.

▼ **FOUR HATS GAME (pages 70–71)**

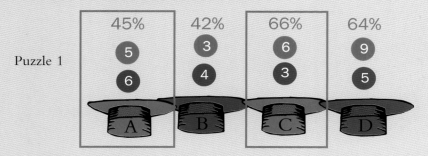

Puzzle 1

The probability that you will choose a red chip is highest when you
choose the chips from the two red hats as shown above.

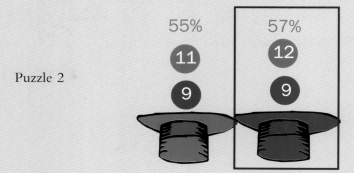

Puzzle 2

By combining the chips in two hats, the surprising outcome is that now
you have to choose from the blue hat in order for you to have your best
chance of drawing a red chip. The paradox can arise in actual research. It
is usually caused by a combination of a lurking variable and data from
unequally sized groups combined into a single data set. It can be avoided
in carefully designed experiments.

### DROWNING IN THE LAKE (page 72)

Being told the average depth does not provide a complete description of the depth of the lake. We must also know something about the variations in depth.

If 3/4 of the lake was 1 foot deep, and the other quarter of the lake was 9 feet deep—deep enough for Ernie to drown in—that would still average three feet.

### THE PROBLEM OF X (page 73)

Your intuitive reaction would be to give an answer of 10. But in this case if x were 9, the percentage error would be greater than 10%.

Therefore, if you are guessing the value of x with a penalty for percentage error, it would be a better guess to choose 9.9. That gives a maximum percentage error of 10% for any value of x—it's 0.9 off from 9, and 1.1 off from 11.

### PREDICTING EARTHQUAKES (page 74)

She predicted that there would be a major earthquake every day over 365 days.

### LOOK IN THE TUBE (page 75)

As you keep staring, the direction from which you see the person at the end of the tube will change.

▼ **TRIPLE DUEL (page 76)**

This puzzle is an example of game theory, which was born in 1927, when John von Neumann recognized that certain decision-making situations in economics, politics, warfare, and other fields are mathematically equivalent to certain games of strategy. Lessons earned from such games can be directly applied in real–life situations. Neumann teamed up with Oskar Morgenstern, an economist, to publish *Theory of Games and Economic Behavior.*

Many of the results of game theory are counterintuitive. For instance, amazingly, Mike's chances of survival are twice as good as those of Tom and Bill! Why?

Tom and Bill will obviously shoot at each other first (as representing the greater threat) and Mike will then have the first shot at the survivor, with a 50% chance of hitting him (and so being the overall winner), and a 50% of missing (and so being shot himself).

Now comes the interesting part.

If Mike has the first shot he must fire into the air, for if he kills either Tom or Bill then the other will kill him.

So there are really only two cases to consider:

Tom shoots first and kills Bill, or vice versa.

In each case Mike has a 50% of hitting the survivor, so his overall probability of surviving is 1/2.

Tom's chance is 1/2 if he shoots first, but 0 if Bill shoots first. Since there is a 50% chance Bill will shoot first, Tom's overall probability of survival is $1/2 \times 1/2 = 1/4$, with Bill having the same probability.

**TARGET SHOOTING (page 77)**

The probability that the target will not be hit is:

$3/5 \times 6/10 \times 7/10 = 0.252$

Therefore, the probability that it will be hit is:

$1 - 0.252 = 0.748$

### SCATTERHEAD (page 78)

Counting the number of randomly appearing beads shown in the windows of Scatterhead over the course of six steps of the experiment, we get the following result:

> red: 31
> green: 6
> yellow: 7
> blue: 16

which is quite a good approximation of the true distribution of 60 colored balls hidden in the box (30 red, 6 green, 9 yellow, 15 blue)

Statistics is a science which studies the collection and meaning of data. Many problems can be solved by statistics. Most such problems are based on uncertainties and incomplete information. Statistics uses samples—i.e., groups of objects selected from a large group under consideration.

A random sample is one picked out by chance. Thus, probability is a very important topic in statistics. Statistics uses polls by means of which estimates are made on the composition of a large group by determining the opinion of a sample.

If we want to consult a large enough sample so that it will reflect the whole "universe" with at least 98% precision, how large does this very reliable sample have to be?

If the universe numbers 200 persons, for example, then the sample must include 105 persons. In the case of 10,000 persons, the sample would have to consist of 213 persons. In case of 100,000 you have to add only 4 to the earlier sample. Essentially, the principle of statistical sampling for larger "universes" is similar to our Scatterhead toy experiment.

Statistics also tells us how much risk we take of being wrong. We reduce the risk by using a large number of samples. If you know something about statistics, you will not be fooled by false statements based on wrong interpretations of data.

Graphs are very useful and are often used in statistics and probability. They visualize numerical facts and quickly summarize relationships of data.

## RABBIT MAGIC (page 79)

The first contestant's hat must have been labeled RRR or RRW. Let's say it was RRR; he could then deduce that, since the label was wrong, the third rabbit was white.

The second contestant's hat must therefore have held one red and two white rabbits and been labeled RRW (so he could deduce the color of the third rabbit). Of the two remaining labels, whichever was on the third hat, the third contestant would be able to deduce the color of the third rabbit (red if the label were WWW; white if it were RWW); we are told he cannot determine the color of the third rabbit, so this is impossible. So the first hat must be labeled RRW and contain three red rabbits.

This leaves RWW as the only possible label for the second hat; it contains two red rabbits and one white one. If the third hat were labeled WWW, the contestant would know the color of the third rabbit, so his hat is labeled RRR. The fourth contestant's hat is labeled WWW, and of the two possible sets of rabbits remaining (WWW or RWW), the correct one must be one red and two white rabbits. The third hat therefore contains three white rabbits.

## BIRTHDAY PROBLEMS (page 80)

Puzzle 1) Most people guess that the answer to this question is 150 or more. The actual answer may surprise you.

With only 23 people in a randomly selected group, the odds of two having the same birthday are better than 50-50. The reasoning is as follows: The odds that two people will have different birthdays is 364/365. (The first person can have any birthday, and the second can have any of the other 364.) A third person can have one of the remaining 363 days. The odds of this happening are $(364/365) \times (363/365)$.

The probability of having the same birthday increases as the probability of having different birthdays diminishes. When you think about the problem combinatorially, among the 23 people there are really 253 possible pairings, making it more believable that such a small number of people is sufficient.

$(364/365) \times (363/365) \times ........ \times ([365-n + 1]/365)$

where n is the total number of people.

The total number of pairings among n people:

$n \times (n - 1)/2$ which equals

$1 + 2 + 3 + ..... + n - 1$.

Puzzle 2) The answer is 253.

The probability of a coincidence is $1 - (364/365)^n$ where n is the number of people besides yourself.

▼ **GLOVES IN THE DARK (page 81)**

To answer the problem we have to consider the worst scenario in which I may be unlucky enough to draw all the left-handed or all the right-handed gloves, of each of which there are 14 gloves.

In such a case, the 15th drawn glove will form a complete pair.

But I can do better than that, since though it is completely dark I can distinguish between left and right-handed gloves. In this case, the worst scenario would be to choose 13 right- or left-handed gloves and then choose one more of the other handed group of gloves to have a perfect pair, making it necessary for me to chose only 14 gloves total.

The two scenarios are depicted below.

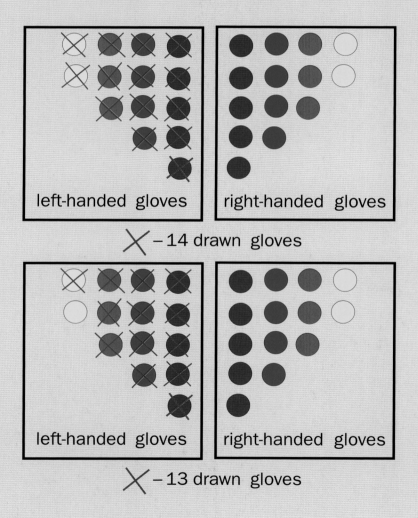

left-handed gloves    right-handed gloves

✗ – 14 drawn gloves

left-handed gloves    right-handed gloves

✗ – 13 drawn gloves

## SOCKS IN THE DARK (page 82)

To ensure having a pair of socks of any color I must draw 4 socks.

To ensure having a pair of each color, I must draw all the socks of two colors (14 socks) and then two more socks, making 16 socks altogether.

## LOST SOCKS (page 83)

The total number of ways to make a pair of socks (matched or unmatched) out of a set of 20 socks is 190. You can check this on your own: write the numbers 1–20 on a piece of paper. There are 19 numbers which you could pair up with the number 1. Now cross out the 1 (since you've already accounted for all the pairs that include it) and look at the 2. There are 18 numbers left that haven't yet been paired with the 2, so add 18 to 19 (making 37 possible pairs of socks so far), cross out the 2, and continue in this fashion until you get to the last pair. You'll end up with this equation:

19 + 18 + 17 + 16 + 15 + 14 + 13 + 12 + 11 + 10 + 9 + 8 + 7 + 6 + 5 + 4 + 3 + 2 + 1 = 190.

We already know that the 20 socks match up evenly, so there are 10 matching pairs of socks. This means that of the 190 possible combinations, 10 match and 180 do not. So it is 18 times more likely that the worst-case scenario will occur, and there will be only 8 remaining pairs of socks that match.

## ▶ NEON SPREADING ILLUSION (page 85)

Tilting the page at a 45-degree angle causes the illusion to disappear.

### ▼ BROKEN STICK (page 86)

The equilateral triangle provides an elegant geometrical analogy to solving the problem. Each point in the triangle represents a unique way to break the stick. The sum of the three perpendiculars (P) is constant and equal to the altitude of the triangle, which is the length of the stick (L).

The three lines will form a triangle only when the point indicating how the stick is broken falls inside the small middle triangle. In such a case none of the three perpendiculars will be longer than the sum of the other two, which is a necessary condition of forming a triangle.

On the other hand, if the point is outside the middle triangle, one perpendicular is sure to be longer than the sum of the other two.

Since the area of this triangle is 1/4 of the total area of the big triangle, the probability of the broken walking stick forming a triangle is also 1/4.

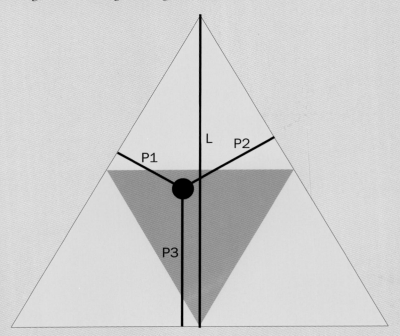

### ▶ PRIVATE EYE (page 87)

This is one of the variations of the classic Necker cube reversal illusion.

The moment of rearrangement that takes place when the wall with the keyhole reverses itself is like a rotation through the fourth dimension.

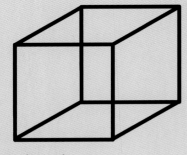

Necker cube

## RANDOM WALK (page 88)

Probability theory says that after n flips, the walker will be, on average, a distance of $\sqrt{n}$ away from the starting point at the middle. For 36 flips this distance would be six marks left or right of the midpoint.

Despite this, the chance of eventually returning to the start is 100%, though it may take a long time to happen.

A very interesting question that arises here is, "How often is the walker likely to change sides?"

Because of the walk's symmetry, one would expect that in a long random walk, the walker would spend about half of his time on each side of the starting point. Exactly the opposite is true! The most probable number of changes from one side to the other is zero.

## RANDOM DRUNKARD'S WALK (page 89)

We really cannot say where the drunkard will be at the end of his walk, but we can answer the question about his most probable distance from the lamppost after a given number of flips.

The most probable distance D from the lamppost after a certain large number of irregular turns is equal to the average length of each straight track of the walk L, times the square root of their total number N:

$$D = L \times \sqrt{N}$$

For example, if the lengths of moves along the grid are of a unit length, after 100 flips of the two coins the drunkard's probable distance from the lamppost would be ten units.

The drunkard will eventually get back to the safety of the lamppost with certainty on a two-dimensional finite square grid.

When there are no barriers and the random walk is not finite the situation becomes quite complex, giving rise to many unsolved problems and theories.

The situation is even more complex in a 3-dimensional random walk along a finite space lattice. The big surprise here is that a random walker is practically certain to reach any intersection in a finite time. In practical terms, if you are inside a large building or a maze with a very complex network of corridors and passages, you can be sure of reaching an exit in a finite time by walking randomly through the structure.

But if the lattice is infinite, however, this is not the case.

▼ **WHO TELLS THE TRUTH?** (pages 90–91)

▼ **NONTRANSITIVE DICE (pages 92–93)**

Die A beats die B, die B beats die C, die C beats die D, and die D beats die A.

The game has a circular winning arrangement, which can best be worked out by creating score charts of all possible encounters between two dice in the set.

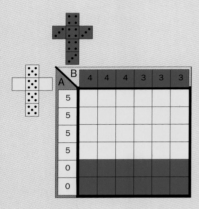

A beats B with a probability of 0.66

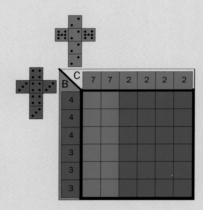

B beats C with a probability of 0.66

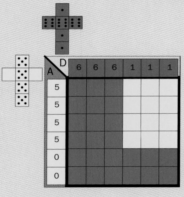

B equals D with a probability of 0.50

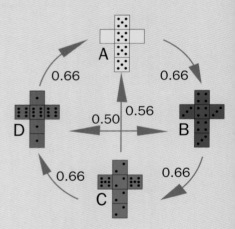

D beats A with a probability of 0.66

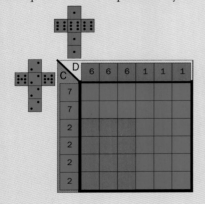

C beats D with a probability of 0.66

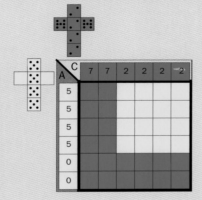

C beats A with a probability of 0.56

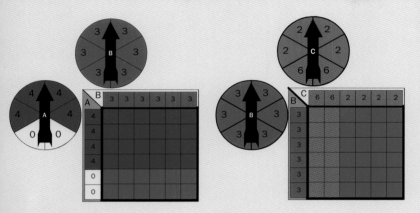

A beats B with a probability of 0.66     B beats C with a probability of 0.66

◄ **NONTRANSITIVE SPINNERS 1 (pages 94)**

When any two spinners are playing against each other, there are 36 possible outcomes. For instance, taking spinner A and B, we can see that 24 times out of 36, A will show value 4, therefore beating the value 3 of B (which will appear 36 times out of 36).

With B and C, spinner C will spin a two 24 times, allowing B to win.

The results are shown in diagrammatic form at left. You can see that C beats D 24 times out of 36 and D beats A with the same frequency, another nontransitive paradox.

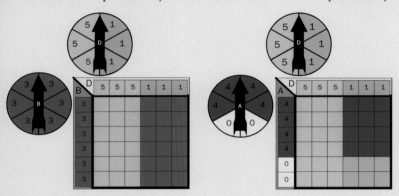

B ties A with a probability of 0.50     D beats A with a probability of 0.66

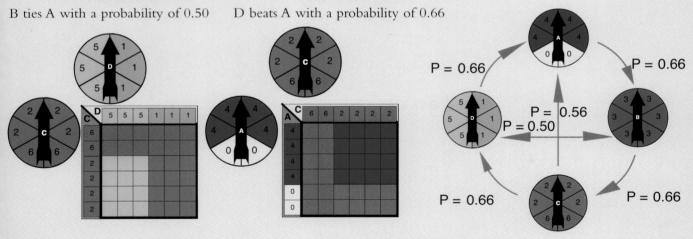

C beats D with a probability of 0.66     C beats A with a probability of 0.56

## ▶ NONTRANSITIVE SPINNERS 2 (page 95)

Mike and Tom are equally matched and so are Mike and Alice. Intuitively you might think that Tom and Alice should be equally matched too. But this is not the case, since Alice beats Tom, as you can see in the charts of possible game outcomes below. Alice is therefore likely to win more games then Tom and Mike in the long run.

| Mike | Tom | Mike | Alice | Tom | Alice |
|------|-----|------|-------|-----|-------|
| 10 | 6 | 10 | 8 | 6 | 8 |
| 10 | 2 | 10 | 4 | 6 | 4 |
| 0 | 6 | 0 | 8 | 2 | 8 |
| 0 | 2 | 0 | 4 | 2 | 4 |

## ▼ NONTRANSITIVE SPINNERS 3 (page 96)

In a series of spins, with each spinner matched against one another, spinner A is the most successful.

Out of 100 spins between A and B, spinner A beats spinner B 56 times. This is because value 2 occupies 56% of the area of spinner B and so whenever the pointer of spinner B registers 2, spinner A, with value 3, wins.

Similarly, spinner A also beats spinner C, but only 51 times out of 100, as 51% of spinner C has a value less than spinner A. Spinner B beats spinner C 66 times out of 100. If all spinners compete simultaneously, however, the chances of spinner A winning are dramatically reduced; in fact it is the worst choice. Look at the graph below of the possible outcomes of a match between B and C; the only way A can win is if B spins a 2 and C spins a 1:

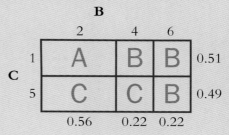

So A's odds of winning are 0.56 × 0.51; B's odds are 2(0.51 × 0.22) + (0.49 × 0.22), and C's are (0.56 + 0.22) × 0.49. Out of 100 spins, A will win 29 times, B will win 33 times, and C will win 38 times.

## LUCKY CARNIVAL SPINNERS (page 97)

The amount of money you can expect to win at any game is called the expected value, and can be calculated by multiplying the potential reward by its likelihood, summed over every outcome.

Doing this for each spinner in turn:

Spinner 1: ($16 × 50%) + ($4 × 50%) = $10.
Spinner 2: ($10 × 50%) + ($8 × 25%) + ($20 × 25%) = $12.
Spinner 3: ($4 × 50%) + ($8 × 25%) + ($16 × 12.5%) + ($28 × 12.5%) = $9.50.
Spinner 4: ($14 × 25%) + ($6 × 25%) + ($6 × 25%) + ($16 × 25%) = $10.50.
Spinner 5: ($0 × 25%) + ($20 × 50%) + ($10 × 25%) = $12.50.

Therefore, spinner 5 is the best choice. For each $10 game you play, on average you will win back $12.50.